Hope Restored

100 Days Through Grief

To Becky,
May the Lord bless you and comfort
you as you read this book. God
is nearby to those that call upon
his name.
            God bless you.
            Hannah Fairchild

Hannah C. Fairchild

O&U
Onwards & Upwards

Onwards and Upwards Publishers

4 The Old Smithy,
London Road,
Rockbeare,
EX5 2EA,
United Kingdom.
www.onwardsandupwards.org

First edition, published in the United Kingdom by Onwards and Upwards Publishers (2020).

ISBN: 978-1-78815-524-3
Typeface: Sabon LT

About the Author

Hannah C. Fairchild is a Belgian poet and writer in her 30s. She is multilingual, having grown up in different countries, and achieved a BSc Honours degree in Psychology. Currently she is living on the Isle of Wight. Though seemingly well prepared for life, tragedy struck her hard and turned her world upside down, when her three children died one after the other.

In the midst of this grief she experienced God's comfort, care and solace. Hannah powerfully put her unspeakable pain into words with her first book, *Sebby*, giving a voice to all who have suffered the loss and grief of a loved one. Her passion is to share her walk with God with others, so that they may be encouraged, comforted and not alone in their pain.

In her second book, *Hope Restored*, she will take you on a journey – honest, heartfelt and one step at a time. It is the journey through grief – never easy, yet still possible with the almighty God at our side.

Join Hannah on her journey to be restored in Christ. Find yourself comforted by her words and insights that resonate with your own experience. Let her faith encourage you in your own walk of faith. Let the mother of three darling children inspire you to have your hope restored.

To contact the author or to order her first book, *Sebby*, please write to *hannahcfairchild@gmail.com.*

More information about the author can be found
on the book's web page:

www.onwardsandupwards.org/hope-restored

Sometimes you have to listen to the
soft voice of courage and say,

'I'll try again tomorrow.'

'Return to your stronghold, O
prisoners of hope, today I declare
that I will restore to you double.'

Zechariah 9:12 (ESV)

'The Lord is close to the broken hearted
and saves those who are crushed in spirit.'

Psalm 34:18 (NIV)

In memory of
Sebastian-David
&
Dad Coleman

*To Carol, Fern, Ronnie and Ashton,
and to my dearest Lee.*

*May the Lord bless you as you navigate through the abyss of
grief. Know that God is with you every step of the way.*

Foreword by Jonathan Snell

I RECOMMEND HANNAH'S BOOK TO ALL WHO EITHER confront the pain of bereavement themselves or are seeking to understand the process of coping with it. She has written with honesty from hard-won personal experience of the loss of her child. There are valuable insights here for the thoughtful reader which are not merely academic or theoretical or oversimplified; they are practical and positive because Hannah diaries a journey which travels out of despair to a place of acceptance. She is straightforward about her good days and bad days while charting a realistic learning curve which gradually moves upwards. Her awareness and acknowledgement of the complex mix of emotions following loss, allied to her determination to move forwards, makes a compelling and helpful read.

Jonathan Snell
Elder
Newport Congregational Church
Isle of Wight

Foreword by Carol Coleman

I AM HONOURED TO BE ASKED BY HANNAH TO WRITE A FEW words. I have been shown love and enlightenment through these writings. My honest belief is that this book will have a profound impact on people who have suffered a great loss. My journey through these pages began on 31st March 2020 when my wonderful husband of 38 years, Brian, was taken by our Lord.

Through Hannah's pain and her journey of loss and bewilderment at the passing of her baby son Sebastian, through prayer and the realisation that our Father God is with us in all trials and tribulations, she was able to put pen to paper and share the ways of our Almighty Father. I was able to overcome my grief, and find strength in His love and her words of encouragement.

My personal journey with our Lord has just started, and Hannah, you are an inspiration to anyone who reads this book – a true woman of God who has been blessed to be able to put pen to paper to help others.

I am blessed to have met you albeit via video call and proud to call you my daughter.

Carol Coleman
Grieving wife of Brian Coleman (also known as 'Dad Coleman')

Introduction

AS I WAS SITTING ON A PLANE RECENTLY AN IDEA FORMED in my head: why not write a devotional book to help people through the wilderness? Although there are already many similar books, we really do need people sharing the gospel, sharing what has helped them to overcome their journey through the wilderness. Although I am not academically qualified to speak on grief, I do have a personal story to tell and a powerful testimony of restoration and hope to share with others who are sitting at the crossroads of life. It is a damaged world that we live in.

I once stood at the crossroads not knowing which way to go. I had a choice: go into the wilderness with Jesus as my companion, or veer off track. In the end I chose to enter the wilderness alongside my companion Jesus. By the grace of God, I emerged at the other end. No, I did not end up in a ditch somewhere; and no, I did not walk away from God. It is always better to serve the Lord than to live without Him.

The grief journey is not just for people who have lost a loved one, but also for those who have lost a dream, or a childhood, or anything that was dear to them. Perhaps you will find some answers in this book.

How to approach this book

This is a 100-day devotional book, so I would recommend taking your time reading it. Maybe skim-read it first. Then go through it a day at a time and work your way from beginning to end.

Take your time with each thought. Draw close to God. Pray out loud or meditate on the Word at your own pace. Don't run from God. Embrace the wilderness. Run to Him and He will answer your needs. He will meet you where you least expect to be met. He will comfort you. He will show you grace. He will bring healing and peace.

Underline! I would encourage you to do this. Underlining what you read can help you engage with the material. Also, when you look back through the book, it is a great way to recap the main points.

In places I reiterate and reinforce the points that I have made, for my own benefit as well as for yours! I believe that repetition can be beneficial.

And as this book will be digested slowly, important points that are repeated will be understood from a different perspective as you progress.

Ideally, read this book through twice. Even though the title is *100 Days Through Grief,* it takes much longer to go through the grief cycle. Grief is a journey that needs to be embarked upon. It is a journey that needs to be embraced. Not something to run away from. God will meet you when you least expect it.

Give yourself some breathing space; allow time for the words of this book to sink in and penetrate your soul so that you can come to a place of healing. Listen to music. For me, it was Christian music that helped me to see hope in a very dark place and helped me to be confident that I would get through it. So, let me encourage you: you *will* get through this. Keep moving forward, pressing into God, drawing close to Him, and He will give you peace.

As I understand it, there are five stages of grief: denial, anger, bargaining, depression and acceptance. I have included devotionals covering these five stages. There's a healthy way of going forward, and an unhealthy way. If you suppress your emotions, you will simply bury your feelings alive, and they will resurface and come to haunt you many years later. They will form a root of bitterness.

God uses trials and tribulations to shape us into the person He wants us to be. Have confidence in God to get you through everything. It is best to deal with grief head-on so that you can move forward. Take it by the horns and let God come into your life and heal you. God wants all His children to draw near to Him, to seek His presence and to feel at peace. He wants us to be free, to be whole.

I would encourage you to read the Bible daily and write one or more encouraging Bible verses in a small book that you can carry around with you throughout the day. Read it when those negative thoughts start to invade your mind. Use it as a weapon against the enemy. When you are at your most vulnerable the enemy can find cracks and come in and ensnare you and take you away from the truths of the Bible. The Word of God is your best weapon, along with prayer, worshipping the Lord and, above all, spending time every day with Him. I want to encourage you to spend time with Father daily. Father God knows all about your future, your plans and your will (both general and specific). Trust Father God for His purpose to be accomplished. Daily time with Him can be an hour or it can be longer. Surrender your struggles to God. Lift your hands in praise. Sing to the Lord. Seek His face. Pray to Him. Worship Him.

Dwell in the safety of His wings. Nail your struggles to the Cross so that you can be free. It is most important to spend time with Father God daily so that you can be healed, so that He can love you. So that he can make you whole.

You will get through this.

You can be a vulnerable person, but you do not need to be a victim to grief. You can learn from it and become stronger. Seek the Lord's presence every day till you are free!

Prologue

WHY HAVE I WRITTEN THIS BOOK? AS WELL AS IT BEING therapeutic for me, I believe that God has called me to write and share His word and to spread the gospel to the nations; to help people know that they are not alone *in the darkness.* The wilderness can be a tough place for us. Even standing on one's feet can be difficult. But if you should crawl, crawl forward not backward. Please do not give up the fight! God is fighting with you. Father is with you all the time. All you need to do is call to Him and He will hear your cry and answer you. Even without you realising it, during your darkest moments God is the one who carries you.

During your wilderness journey, you may think like the psalmist David did:

> *You have taken from me friend and neighbour – darkness is*
> *my closest friend.*
>
> Psalm 88:18 (NIV)

Darkness does not have to be your closest friend. In fact, during the storm in your life it is Jesus who is your closest friend. He hears your cry. It is Father God who weeps with you. It is Jesus who died on the Cross for our sins so that we may have eternal life. Jesus knows our pain and does not want us to suffer. Turn your eyes towards Jesus and He will ultimately give you peace.

> *Let the beloved of the Lord rest secure in him, for he shields*
> *him all day long and the one the Lord loves rests between his*
> *shoulders.*
>
> Deuteronomy 33:12 (NIV)

> *In my distress, I called to the Lord: I cried to my God for*
> *help. From His Temple, He heard my voice, my cry came*
> *before Him, into His ears.*
>
> Psalm 18:6 (NIV)

Do not lose hope. Things will get better. There is an end in sight. The pain will eventually subside, and you'll be able to pick up the disintegrated fragments of your life and stick them back into place with the help of our Father.

There are so many hurting, bewildered people who need the Father – people who are afraid to put their trust in Him; maybe because of some deep tragedy that occurred in their lives. I know that when I lost my son, I was afraid to trust God again. It was a long, arduous journey, but in the end worth all the effort. A journey worth it despite my wavering trust in God; He helped me to pull through and I stand firm in my faith.

My Story

MY JOURNEY TO FAITH HAD BEEN A LONG, ARDUOUS ONE, however rewarding. I became a Christian at the age of fifteen when I attended a Christian Youth Group in Bratislava, Slovakia. For a long time I believed that I would never match up to Christian standards and be like all those people that appeared to live perfect lives and seemed to have no issues at all. How wrong I was! I have come to realise that every one of us has challenges to face, but because of my brokenness I believed that I was the only one that was suffering and not worthy to be a Christian. And because I believed I wasn't worthy of being a Christian, I only half-heartedly believed in God. I was quite reserved in my faith and didn't go all into it. I didn't embrace it completely because a part of me was afraid. It was the echo in my head that said I wasn't good enough to be a Christian which made my walk with God very challenging in the beginning.

I lost three children: Micheline, Elouise and Sebastian-David ('Sebby'). My brother also lost his son David to stillbirth. All these losses had a significant impact on me and also my family, especially after we lost David and Sebastian-David. This then gave me a desire to reach out to people who struggle. As a child/young teenager I never believed that stillbirth and miscarriage could happen to me. I heard about other people facing these challenges but never once did I think that this would be a possibility in my life. I, for some reason, had a belief that when I became an adult life would be easy – with zero challenges. How naïve I was.

With the first two children I had a miscarriage at twelve weeks and four to five months into the pregnancy. This was challenging. But I managed to cope with it by burying my head in the sand. It was only after I ended up in a women's shelter because of an abusive husband that I realised that the way my life was going, things would not improve unless I made drastic changes to it. I made mistakes throughout my young adult life because I wanted to be independent. I didn't want to rely on anyone, not even God. This didn't help and I ended up in some difficult situations which I could have avoided if I had decided to follow the advice of my family, and of the Bible and my church family. Hard lessons were learnt. But it is these lessons that have made me the person that I am today.

I realised I didn't want to allow my past to have such a huge impact on my present and future. I needed to change. But how do you change unless you have a willing heart to change; unless you want a heart of change? Only God can change you when you allow him to take the steering wheel of your life, allow Him to guide you every step of the way. This was my driving force – my willingness to change. When I lived in the shelter in the UK, that is where I believe the foundation of my faith was built on. Shortly after moving into the shelter, I felt the Lord tell me that I should return home to Slovakia where my parents resided. Towards the end of pregnancy, I went into labour and my mom took me to the hospital in Slovakia, which looked like something out of a communist past. When the doctors told me that my son no longer had a heartbeat, I felt like my world was tumbling around me. However, my newfound faith helped me cope with the death of my son. I was asked early on where I would put my trust. Would I grieve in a positive way or in a negative way? Where and whom would I put my trust in? This question was with me throughout the early days of my grief and was my driving force in turning to the Lord for help rather than the default, which was burying my head in the sand.

We have to learn from our past, and the only way we can do this is to learn from within and be willing to change. Without the desire to change we won't grow as people. We will remain stagnant.

DAY 1

Pray continually.

1 Thessalonians 5:17 (NIV)

"THERE ARE MANY WAYS OF BREAKING A HEART. STORIES were full of hearts being broken by love, but what really broke a heart was taking away its dream – whatever dream that might be."[1]

The grief journey is not just for people who have lost a loved one, but also those for who have lost a dream or a childhood. When the train wreck occurs in our lives, when our world suddenly changes and spins out of control, we pray. Or when we just simply fall into dark folds of depression, we pray for a miracle. We bargain with God. We plead with God: 'Please, I'll do anything for you but please don't take my loved one away.' Sometimes we think that if we can bargain with God, He will by some miracle save the one that is dying. Save our closest loved ones. Remove us from this nightmare. Unfortunately, it doesn't always work that way.

I remember the doctors telling me on that awful dark Friday afternoon that they couldn't find a heartbeat in my baby. I remember praying constantly. That is all I really remember. Praying. Begging God to do something. Begging God to keep my baby alive and hoping that the doctors were lying. You want God to protect you from that pain. You want God to take you away from that pain. You want God to answer you right away – but sometimes He does not. And sometimes when He doesn't answer right away, your faith falters. You curl up in a foetal position and wonder what will happen next. The fact is, God doesn't work that way, He doesn't always answer us at once. Sometimes He will take His time to answer just to see if we will trust Him.

What I came to slowly realise after my son died was that God had a reason, *has* a reason, a purpose for all of this, even though at the time it did not make sense. God tests us to see if we really trust Him and if we will really rely on Him in the toughest battles. God uses difficult

---

[1] *The Patriot,* Pearl Buck (1939)

situations to draw us near to Him so that we can rely on him for our strength.

Was I going to put my trust in God?

What do you do when you are thrown into the middle of the storm? Whom do you trust?

It is better to take refuge in the Lord than to trust in man.

Psalm 118:8

Do you put your trust in God? Back then, when I was in that wilting waiting room of a communist past in Slovakia, I made a conscious effort to hold on to the conviction that God would pull me through the shadow of death as I faced a stronghold of grief which was ready to tear me apart. Know the Lord is your Shepherd. Let Him hear your prayer. Let Him answer you.

Remember: sometimes you have to try to be patient and wait for Him to speak to you. If you are open to hearing His word, by the grace of God you will come through this storm in one piece. You will not be disappointed. God knows what is best for you and what you can go through. He doesn't give you anything that you cannot cope with. Just hold onto Him. Let Him be your anchor in the storm of your life.

Prayer Starter

Dear Father God, thank you for the circumstances that you give us. Help me to embrace this journey of grief. Walk with me as I choose to trust you. Amen.

She is Me

She is me.
She could be you.
Weak. Battered. Bruised.
Resilience. Strength. Faith.

She wants to be seen and heard,
She wants to be healed,
She wants to feel the loving touch of God,
She wants grace,
She wants to be forgiven,
She wants to be whole.

Love is tinged by manipulation,
Hope is coloured with pain (from a forgotten past),
Faith is shadowed by uncertainty,
Life is clouded by constant misbeliefs;
But God gave us the Cross
Where we can put our hurts
And where healing can occur.

Does she decide to live by faith?
Or by fear...?
Will she live her life for Him?
Or will she choose to live life for herself?

Self-doubt, the enemy of the soul...
God's certainty should be the lover of her soul.
Why is there so much distrust? So much pain?

Pain, needless pain.
Fear of being alone.
She is me.
She could be you.
Weak. Battered. Bruised.
Resilience. Strength. Faith.

She lives her life by
Resilience, strength, faith.
Love. Hope. Peace.
This is she. This is me.

DAY 2

*Do not be afraid or discouraged, for the Lord will personally
go ahead of you; He will neither fail you nor abandon you.*

Deuteronomy 31:8 (NLT)

THE WORLD IS RAPIDLY SPINNING OUT OF CONTROL. TRA-
gedy strikes daily, whether it is in your world or your next-door
neighbour's. You never know what the future will hold for you. You
think you know exactly where the future will take you, but do you really?

For example, you are pregnant for nine months. It is normal to bring
a baby home after nine months of pregnancy. It is not normal to leave
that cold, sterile hospital without a baby. If that happens, your world
spins out of control. What do you do? What is going through your mind?

*Do you feel like God has failed you? Abandoned you in your time of
need?* Do you feel like you are battling this all alone? Stop! Turn to
scripture. Read scripture out loud. Let God speak to you. Seek His
presence. Be still before Him.

I remember reading Deuteronomy 31:8 and finding the courage to
keep walking straight ahead with my eyes fixed on the Cross. It was all I
could do to focus on the task at hand. Yes, there were times when I was
deeply discouraged. There were also times when I questioned the mere
existence of God. But by reading this Bible verse I was reminded that God
is bigger, and the greatest comforter of all. I received comfort amidst this
trial. This verse reminded me that God is there for me and He will carry
me through the toughest trials. You do not need to face these trials by
yourself. God is holding your hand, sometimes carrying you through as
you face the blistering pain that is plaguing your soul.

You learn to seek the presence of the Lord and be still before Him.
The greatest comfort I found was knowing that God knows what will
happen in my life. God has a perfect plan, and sometimes God uses bad
experiences to draw us near to Him so that we can come to rely on Him
alone. Not just in a crisis but also when we are going through still waters.
God is our anchor. God never changes from east to west, from north to
south. He remains steadfastly the same. This is our greatest comfort. We

know that God never changes like shifting shadows. If we call unto Him, He will answer our prayers in His perfect timing.

Prayer Starter

Dear Father God, please still the world around me. Help me to focus in on you. Help me to cling on to you. Help me to seek your presence and to have the courage to face this grief journey. Amen.

DAY 3

Be joyful in hope, patient in affliction, faithful in prayer.

Romans 12:12 (NIV)

DO YOU OFTEN FEEL HOPELESS? FULL OF DESPAIR? WHEN people are going through spiritual trenches, there is tendency to lose their faith. We tend to rely on our own strength, push away the things that are closest to us. What we really need, down at the muddy bottom of this trench, is to cling onto our God for guidance.

Your word is a lamp for my feet, a light on my path.

Psalm 119:105

We should always cling to God for guidance. We should always point our eyes towards the Cross where all healing can occur.

To defeat the enemy, we need to have our roots firmly planted and strongly rooted into the ground. Then, whatever suffering we may endure, we can combat with God's word. We can fight it with 'the helmet of salvation and the sword of the Spirit, which is the word of God'[2].

Remember: the word of God is alive and active, sharper than a double-edged sword.[3]

If we read the word of God daily, and pray daily, then we are ready to rise above any affliction that faces us. We can use the truths of God to fight against the lies of the enemy.

Praying daily to our Father is important. It opens communication channels between you and Him. It creates an open relationship with Him, filled with compassion, love, grace, mercy, forgiveness and so much more.

Allow yourself to be joyful in every situation. Allow yourself to be content with whatever you are facing, knowing that the Lord your God is with you and that His love will see you through each and every difficulty you face.

---

[2] See Ephesians 6:17
[3] See Hebrews 4:12

Prayer Starter

Dear Father God, help me to have hope. Fill me with your peace. Fill me with your love. Help me to sing to you with praises. Amen.

DAY 4

'For I know the plans I have for you,' declares the Lord,
'plans to prosper you, and not to harm you, plans to give
you hope and a future.'

Jeremiah 29:11 (NIV)

IT IS HARD TO UNDESTAND HOW GOD HAS EVERYTHING under control, considering there are millions of people walking on the planet, and how God has a plan for each one of us. How amazing and tough is that! Tough to get your head around it, because when you are spiritually in a rut you can feel shakily insecure in your faith; after an earthquake has hit your world, you wonder where God was in all of it. You begin to wonder whether God is really out there.

Sound familiar? I really struggled with the notion that God knew every aspect of my life and that He knew what was best for me. In my head, I was thinking:

'Eh, really... umm, I don't think so.'

Specifically, after the earth-shattering moment when they told me, 'Your son's heartbeat is gone,' I could not possibly understand how this was in God's plan. Or how this could be a better plan. But I had to trust Him. I had to put my confidence in Him, and that He knew what was best for me. God knows what we can cope with.

The one thing I have learnt on my wilderness journey is this: *God can turn tragedy into something beautiful. And it is so.*

All we need to do is trust God to carry us through the storm; to allow Him to enter our world of sin. We must believe that God's plan is far better than the plans that we thought were best for us. Sometimes, that means not understanding why some catastrophic event happens in our lives, but simply accepting it. It means that we don't always have to understand, but that we simply must learn to trust and not question the whys and what-ifs.

Prayer Starter

Dear Lord, help me to focus on Your plans, not the plans that I have for my future. Fill me with Your desires for me and help me to follow your righteous path. Amen.

DAY 5

He will cover you with his feathers, and under his wings you will find refuge; His faithfulness will be your shield and rampart.

Psalm 91:4 (NIV)

DURING GRIEF, PAIN, LOSS, CONFLICT AND ANGER, I QUICKLY learnt that Father God covered me with His feathers and gave me rest when I needed it most. Father God carried me through relentless crashing waves when I couldn't carry on anymore. Sometimes He would carry me, other times He would walk beside me and encourage me as if I were a small child trying to walk. Maybe in many ways I was learning to walk again. It certainly felt like that at times.

I learnt quickly by experience that when you call on Him, He will hear you and make His dwelling within you. Maybe it sounds too easy?

What do you do when you are going through the barren desert? Do you run a hundred miles away or do you seek God and ask Him to come into your life, so that you can experience healing? If you run, why do you run from Him? Are you scared? And if so, what are you scared of?

I used to fear what God thought of me. I used to think that I was not good enough, but I learnt that as Father God's child I could run to Him at any time. Father God wants His children to run to Him so that we may find our peace in Him. He can be our protector when things go wrong. He can be our healer, our counsellor even in times of deep trouble.

Don't be afraid of the pain that is coursing through your veins but embrace it. Let God in, so that He can be your shield and rampart. He can fight the battles for you, the ones that you cannot battle on your own.

Prayer Starter

Dear Lord, please fill me with your love. Help me to seek your presence as I try to figure out what I am afraid of. Help me to have faith, and take away any fear that I have. I trust in you, Father. Heal me, please, I pray. Amen.

DAY 6

*Therefore I tell you, whatever you ask for in prayer, believe
that you have received it, and it will be yours.*

Mark 11:24 (NIV)

ONE DAY I WAS SITTING IN THE CAR, FEELING LIKE A
completely hopeless case; not sure how to keep going, or even how to
park the car in the so-called *garage*. I was a beginner. So, I prayed to
Father God.

'Father God, please help me to park this car in this so-called *garage!*
I really don't know how to do this. Lord, you are in control of this vehicle
and I trust that you will help me.'

And sure enough, He answered me and helped me to park my car. In
the same way, we can apply this simple principle to every aspect of our
lives. It does not always mean that Father God will answer our prayers
right away, but He does answer them in His timing.

Sometimes you just have to pray and surrender to God, and let him
take the steering wheel of your broken vehicle and lead you onto the right
road. You have to trust that He will supply what you asked Him for in
His perfect timing. You have to truly believe that God has the best for
you. Father God will answer our prayers within reason if it is what He
wants for us. If it is not what He wants for us, He will give us something
better along the way.

Surrender yourself to Him. Surrender your struggles to Him. Let go,
so that you can be free. Seek God's presence, pray to Him, worship Him,
praise Him even when the going gets tough. Your biggest asset in your
wretched grief journey is knowing who is greater than your problems and
knowing who can comfort you when no-one else can.

Prayer Starter

*Dear Lord, you are a gracious God, a compassionate God. You know
what is best for me. Help me to surrender my struggles to the Cross. Fill
me up with the Holy Spirit. Heal me. Help me to spend more and more
time in your presence, as I learn all about you, even when I don't always*

understand why this tragedy had to happen. I am choosing to trust you, that you know what is best for me. Amen.

DAY 7

Come to me, all you who are weary and burdened and I will
give you rest.

Matthew 11:28 (NIV)

DO YOU FEEL LIKE YOU ARE HAVING A BURNOUT? OR LIKE you are constantly overwhelmed? Or depressed? Lonely? Afraid? Tired? Unsure? Uncertain?

Then the right place for you is at the foot of the Cross where you can lay every single burden down. Nail it to the Cross. Allow God's love to seep through your bones. Allow Father God to speak to you. Find rest. Find peace. Be still before Him. But don't continue to live life in rollercoaster mode until you crash to a standstill and realise you have hit rock bottom with no way of going on.

Sometimes in the Christian walk you must be still before Him and let others serve you; at other times you are the one that is doing the serving. Don't feel guilty when you can't serve in the usual way. Sometimes you just need to rest in the presence of Father God.

When we are feeling emotionally unstable, or have a raging storm within us, it is always good to present those emotions to the Cross. Especially the ones that drag us under; the ones that fester into a fiery ball of angst. 'On this Cross, Lord, I present you with my anxieties: fear, rejection, abandonment, being unlovable, low self-esteem, wounded spirit, self-hatred, bitterness, anger, frustration.'

I used to draw a Cross and pin every struggle on that Cross. By writing it down, in a way I was releasing it. I was acknowledging that I had struggles. And by drawing a Cross and writing my struggles on the Cross, I was enabling myself to let go of things that bound me in besetting sin.

Prayer Starter

Dear Lord, please Lord, help me to overcome all these negative emotions within my broken soul. Draw me closer to you, oh Lord. Oh Lord, please hear my cry. Lord, help me to find rest in you. Amen.

DAY 8

Peace I leave with you; my peace I give you. I do not give as the world gives. Do not let your hearts be troubled, and do not be afraid.

John 14:27 (NIV)

NEW SITUATIONS CAN SCARE US, AND SOMETIMES EVEN WE believers can turn away from God during uncertain times because we do not know if we can trust God to see us through.

But can we get through a difficult situation in our own strength? Or do we run a thousand miles from our difficult situation only to find ourselves in another ditch? I have learnt the hard way, that God would much rather we ran to Him, so that He can help us through difficult situations and guide us to a place of safety.

Sometimes, it is certainly easier to run away from the pain, the grief, those all-consuming emotions. But it isn't always – or necessarily – healthy. If you bury those emotions and your troubles, they remain buried and will become a festering hot ball of fire, ready to explode any moment. That is unhealthy.

Eventually, it will catch up with you. Will you run away from it again? Or will you face it? Which is easier – to let Father God in and to let Him heal you from the inside out, or to let it consume you? It is much easier to let Father God heal you and shower you with His love. Ultimately, He is love. He is a compassionate Father. He is the greatest healer. He gives peace to all those who run to Him in the face of battles and difficulties. Yet He does not just share His peace with us in adversity; He also gives it to us in peaceful times.

God wants us to focus on Him so that He can help us through the murkiness of grief. He doesn't want to see His children suffer. He uses times of difficulty to draw us near to Him, so that we can experience not only the renewal of our minds, but also the peace that transforms our minds.

Prayer Starter

Dear Father God, thank you for the strength that you give me to face each new day. Each day I will sing you praises. Help me to focus on you and not on the problems in front of me. Teach me a new song, oh Lord. Heal me, Lord Jesus. I will trust you. In your most precious name, I pray. Amen.

DAY 9

Wait for the Lord, be strong and take heart and wait for the Lord.

Psalm 27:14 (NIV)

ARE YOU IMPATIENT? I STRUGGLE WITH WAITING! OVER THE years, God has taught me a lot about waiting. Some of the most valuable lessons when I have to wait are:

- how to have peace;
- how to be patient;
- how to keep a relaxed attitude.

Sometimes if you get ahead of yourself and you don't wait, you miss an opportunity. You miss God's best for you. Learn to see waiting as a season of growth, not just as a trial of pain to endure. Change your view on waiting. See it as an opportunity to spend more time with God and to spend more time in His word. Use your time wisely. And do not lose hope!

Just because things don't seem to fall into place quickly does not mean that God isn't working things out for you. He moves according to His own timing, and if it means you must wait, then wait. Don't fight it. Maintain a relaxed attitude. Don't panic just because things don't turn out the way you planned.

Prayer Starter

Dear Lord, please help me to stay focussed on Your goal, Your will for my life. Please help me to have patience to wait. Lord, help me to be at peace while I am waiting for Your best for me. Thank you, Lord. Amen.

In El Shaddai's Presence I sit

In El Shaddai's presence I sit,
With the earth roaring, gripping me into deathly silence.
In the terror of the night I say this:
'You God are my refuge, I trust in you, and I am safe.'
Safe, oh so safe, in the arms of Jesus.
Help me to be still as I seek your presence,
Surrounded by the debris of my broken vessel.
You, God are my God, lover of my soul.
Safe, oh so safe I am, knowing that you are with me,
Calling me, sheltering me under your wings
Of grace, love, compassion, mercy and forgiveness.

DAY 10

*My soul is weary with sorrow, strengthen me according to
your word.*

Psalm 119:28 (NIV)

A LONG TIME AGO WHEN I WAS FEELING SAD, I USED TO TURN
to binge-eating to fill up the emptiness, the holes in my life. I still do
sometimes. I used to wonder why I was not feeling better, and why that
lonely, empty feeling wasn't disappearing. I wondered. I struggled. I
battled with my feelings. I wanted to get better. But somehow it wasn't
working.

I would read the Bible once every few days until one day I decided to
challenge myself and read it every day. Reading the Bible daily was good
for me. It changed my perspective on life, and it started to fill the
emptiness that I was feeling. God's word strengthened me, and it slowly
raised me out of the pit of sorrow – the weariness was lifting. I was slowly
building a relationship with my Father in heaven and He was showing
me the way forward.

His Word was comforting me, and within His Word I found the
strength to carry on. It was mending my broken spirit. In the same way,
God can strengthen you. Let Him into your life, allowing yourself to be
open to His word and to that small inner voice of His Spirit speaking to
you.

I want to encourage you to read the Bible daily. Maybe even write a
Bible verse in a little notebook. Pick a bright colour that encourages you.
When you are feeling low, you can open that book and read the Bible
verses that speak to you repeatedly. Eventually you will find that your
soul, weary with sorrow, will find peace and comfort from God.

Prayer Starter

*Dear Lord, help me to read Your word. Speak to me as I read Your word.
Amen.*

DAY 11

Many are the plans in a person's heart, but it is the Lord's purpose that prevails.

Proverbs 19:21 (NIV)

WE SHOULD NOT UNDERESTIMATE THE POWER OF GOD. I remember a time when I had many plans for my future. I had dreams for my son – dreams to be the best mummy in the world – but the Lord had other plans for my life. For a long time after my son died, I felt like I couldn't make plans. I didn't dare to have plans. I didn't dare to have hope and desires, because I was afraid that those plans would also fail. Only the Lord's plans will succeed, and in order to know what plans are from our heavenly Father, we need to look heavenwards and wait for His soft voice to speak to our hearts. Ultimately, we need to find our peace with the decision we are making for our future.

Though there seems to be a lot of uncertainty about my future, I know that the Lord's purpose will prevail over the purpose I have set out for my life. To trust Him, I need to spend time in a lot of prayer and believe that God puts desires in our hearts that will become a reality one day, unfolding a true story.

There was one time in my life when I knew without a doubt that I was following the Lord's will for my life. Completely at peace with the decision that I had made, I observed God move mountain after mountain in my life, overcoming every obstacle that was being thrown at me. Wow! Just – wow! I was in complete awe at the power of my wonderful, majestic God. That time was a special time for me. I was learning to trust Him, and to get to know Him on a much deeper and more powerful level.

My question for you is, do you allow God to be in control of every aspect of your life? Or do you still try to exert control in certain areas? Unveil yourself before the Cross and allow God to seep in and to lead you onto the right path. Allow God to give you His desires and hopes for your future. Trust Him. Believe that anything is possible. Where there seems to be no way, God the Father always makes a way. So pray, relax in His presence and wait for Him to open the next door for you.

Remember: patience is a virtue. Have patience!

Prayer Starter

Dear Father God, show me your plans for my life. Show me the purpose that you have for my life. Teach me your ways. In you I put my trust. In you I put my hope for a future. Thank you, Lord, for your love and care. Thank you that you are with me and that I do not have to face this alone. Teach me, Lord, your decrees. Teach me to be patient. In your most precious name, I pray. Amen.

DAY 12

The lions may grow weak and hungry, but those who seek
the Lord lack no good thing.

Psalm 34:10 (NIV)

ONE STUPID DECISION AND YOUR LIFE CAN ALTER RADI-
cally. A split second, and suddenly you realise how tenuous life can be;
how this instant focuses our eyes onto an invisible thread between life
and death, between light and darkness, between evil and good. In that
moment you realise your vulnerability, the realisation that evil can walk
alongside you. We feel the constant battle between the desires of the flesh
and of the soul. Life is a challenge. Life is difficult. Is this thing we call
life worth living when every day we hear so much about our own
tendency to evil and to sin?

Today I question, where is God? Why can't He stop all this evil in the
world? What is happening to the world around me? Why is there so much
evil? Why did God give us free will when He knew that it would result in
complete chaos? How can we change the course of our life and make sure
that we don't walk influenced by evil, but that we allow the goodness of
the Lord, of the Holy Spirit, to infiltrate every part of our being? How
can we make sure that we do not fall into the enemy's trap, and make
sure that we walk alongside the Lord and onto His right path? How can
God allow his own people to commit violent acts of crime? How can God
allow people to commit such horrible acts against humanity and not stop
it? How can we overcome this evil and do what is good and pure? What
is the point in this thing called life?

I am just as much a sinner as the person next to me. If I can think
badly of someone, then that makes me not a nice person. The Bible
teaches us to love our enemies as ourselves, to treat people with the
respect and love that they deserve.

I fear my own vulnerability to evil and to sin. Today I realise I do not
want to sin. I want to walk alongside my Father. I want to do what is
good and not evil. I want to seek His presence. In His presence I know
that I am whole. I know that I can be who He wants me to be, the loving
compassionate woman of God He created me to be.

Seek the Lord. Seek his presence. Open that communication channel to create that personal relationship. Do not be afraid to seek Him. But be aware of the danger that lurks about you, for the enemy prowls and is ready to destroy. Keep your helmet of salvation on and be prepared to fight the evil forces around you. Do good and be blessed.

Prayer Starter

Dear Father God, thank you for providing for my needs. Thank you that I am not alone. You are faithful and in you I put my trust. Lead me away from evil. Teach me your ways, oh Lord, I pray. Amen.

DAY 13

What do you mean, 'If I can?' Jesus asked. 'Anything is
possible if a person believes.'

Mark 9:23 (NLT)

IT IS GOD WHO PLANTS PEOPLE IN OUR LIVES, AND IT IS THESE
people who will help us to see our true potential. These people will be
the ones who encourage you and who will be the key motivators to
making your life's dreams come true.

A year ago, I did not believe that I would be able to publish my first
book. Then I met someone who saw my gift for words, saw that I could
have an impact on hundreds of people. This one person was the key to
opening my potential. God provided someone to open that door for me
to release my dream. Instead of discouraging me and dissuading me from
publishing my book, the encouragement has helped to build up my self-
esteem. I saw that they believed in me in the same way that God believed
in me. It was the push that I needed to move in a new but meaningful
direction and onto the path that God has been preparing for me.

This important person gave me a lot of good, encouraging feedback
rather than negative feedback. This positive motivation and gentle
encouragement made me feel loved and recognised, and made me feel like
I am worthy, that my life isn't wasteful and has a potential that I never
thought it had before.

Potential. Success. Hope. Motivation. I am loved. I am not a failure
and I will succeed. There is always hope. I can be an achiever. I can be
an encourager. Through God all things are possible.

Perhaps you have someone in your life who encourages you and
shows you your true potential in God's image? My advice is to hang out
with people who see your potential; people who see you as God sees you,
and who are willing to encourage you until you reach that potential. Do
you have someone like that in your life? Are you someone who can
encourage someone else and show them their potential?

Prayer Starter

Dear Lord, thank you for your love and grace. Thank you for helping me to be the person you want me to be. Please put people on my path who can encourage me, who can motivate me and who see my potential in Christ. Help me to be a positive encourager to others. Thank you. Amen.

DAY 14

Call on me when you are in trouble and I will rescue you.

Psalm 91:15 (NIV)

WHO IS YOUR EMERGENCY CALL? IS IT GOD? IS IT PERHAPS someone close to you? Whom do you call when you are having a crisis? Do you try to solve it by yourself? Do you rely on your own strength? Or do you rely on the strength of God?

I know for a matter of fact that when I am in a crisis, I can no longer rely on my own strength because at the end of the day I will fall deeper into crisis and I will make a bigger mess of it. Then it takes me longer to get out of the crisis than if I rely on God right away. God will help me; God hears my cry and He will gently guide me to a place of safety and give me peace.

The one thing I am a hundred percent certain of is this: *God is my anchor in times of storms and tranquillity.* Over the last couple of years, I have learnt to rely on Him for everything. I mean literally everything.

To rely on Father for everything, you will need to build up a daily conversation with Him, build a relationship with Him. Do this by spending time reading His word and worshipping Him, rather than focusing on your problems. Believe it or not, the Lord will come and rescue you from the lion's den, when you keep holding onto Him.

God loves it when His children call on Him, and He will meet you. He will show you the way forward, He will protect you. God never gives us things that we cannot cope with. God uses trials and tribulations as a time to test us to see whether we will come to Him for help or whether we will rely on our own strength.

Prayer Starter

Dear Lord, please help me to rely on you on every aspect of my life, not just when I am struggling with some issues. Help me to have communion with you. Help me to meet you in that secret place. Lord, be my anchor in all things. Amen.

DAY 15

In this world you shall have tribulation.

John 16:33 (NIV)

SUFFERING, TRIBULATION AND CHALLENGES ARE ALL A PART of life. It is part of what it means to be human in a fallen world. But because we have God in our lives, Christ is our anchor that holds fast in all our storms. However, if we do not sail into the teeth of the gale, how will we know that our Father is a gracious God? A God of compassion? A God who bears the brunt of our suffering? How do we know that, unless we face our trials head-on with zeal and counting it joy?

It is only in times of deepest distress and sorrow that we reach out to Him, when all else has failed. It takes a crisis for us to turn to Him for help. What do we find? God is constant. God never changes from the east to the west, from north to south. When we reach out to God, He is waiting to comfort us and to uphold us through it all. In this way, He proves His faithfulness to us and ensures we will remain close to Him.

The question you should ask yourself is, will you skirt around the storm or sail into the eye of the storm when ultimately you can experience true healing from our Lord and Saviour?

When my son died, I decided that, rather than facing this journey on my own, I would cling onto the only anchor I had – Father God. I decided to find the courage to face what was to be one of the most difficult times in my life. Yet I came through because I had Father God by my side every step of the way.

Perhaps my time in the shelter and my childlike faith helped me to build a trusting relationship with Him, knowing that He would meet my needs and carry the brunt of my suffering even in the darkest moments. I liken my time in the shelter to a training ground for me to learn who God the Father really is. It was a time of intense learning about who He is and learning to be fully dependent on Him. If I had not spent the previous six months learning all about God, I would have been worse off after my son died. Praise the Lord for all the experiences he gives us!

Prayer Starter

Dear Lord, please give me the courage and the strength to face trials and tribulations and all that you have in store for me. Help me to embrace my wilderness and not run from it. Amen.

DAY 16

You who sit in the High God's presence, spend the night in Shaddai's shadow, say this: 'God, You're my refuge. I trust in You and I'm safe!'

Psalm 91:1-2 (MSG)

I SUFFER FROM UNSCRUPULOUS PANIC AND ANXIETY attacks. It used to be on a regular basis, but now it is easing a bit. When I used to have panic/anxiety attacks I would think the absolute worst, and nothing could console me. There was a time when even Father God didn't have first place in my heart. It was a time when everything else was more important. Like looking pretty.

But over time, when the panic/anxiety attacks became more difficult to endure, I knew I had to do something to change that. I challenged myself to write one encouraging Bible verse each day in my little yellow book. Whenever I felt the bile rising in my throat, sweaty palms, etc., I knew I had to whisper God's truths over the enemy's lies that were wreaking havoc in my life.

The secret to overcoming demonic panic/anxiety attacks is by having an endless supply of encouraging Bible verses that will see you through those attacks. That is simply equipping yourself with simple truths from the Bible and praying over yourself as soon as you know you are approaching such an attack.

In fact, a simple exercise I did was to create a table with two columns where I would write down the lies of the enemy in one column and match each one with a truth from the Bible in the other column. It proved to be a good exercise. The enemy could not undermine the presence of Father God in my heart!

You seek God's presence and say, 'Father, You're my refuge. I trust in You and I'm safe.'

Prayer Starter

Dear Father God, you're my refuge. I trust in you and I'm safe. Thank you for your presence. Thank you that I can come before you and lay my burdens down, for your yoke is easy and your burden is light. Amen.

DAY 17

*The Lord is close to the broken-hearted and saves those who
are crushed in spirit.*

Psalm 34:18 (NIV)

CRUSHED, HEARTBROKEN, COMPLETELY LOST IN THE MINE-
field of grief, I felt like I was blinded and that I couldn't see anything.
Father God was my eyes. He guided me, He helped me. He showed me
grace. He showed me compassion. He loved me. The list is endless.

Think of a time when God helped you and was close to you; a time
when you were crushed in spirit when you were completely heartbroken.
What did God do for you? Did you feel His presence?

Learn to lean into Him. Let Him bind up your open wounds. Search
His presence and you will experience fullness of joy and healing like never
before.

Has there ever been a time in your life that you felt like God was so
far away when you were in the middle of the storm? Then, as you slowly
left that storm behind, the veil over your eyes lifted and you saw that
God was beside you the entire time. Isn't that an amazing feeling? It is
such a warm feeling, knowing that you are never alone and that Father
has always got your back.

It is often said that God the Father and Jesus Christ are our closest
confidants and that they never abandon us. It may not feel like that. But
it is God who suffers with us. He hates seeing His children suffer. He
wants us to run to Him, and to share our brokenness with Him. He
doesn't want us to run away from Him. When we run to Him, He can
give us that hope, and show us His will for our life.

What is life, if we only fear? Isn't life better when we have hope, even
if the future is unknown? It is better to live in hope than to be afraid. For
when we have faith we can hope. Faith is the door to believing that
anything is possible, opening our hearts to the light of hope in the darkest
moments of our lives.

Prayer Starter

Dear Lord, please lead me home when I am suffering in silence. Open the door and let me run home to You, so that I can experience hope and not live in fear. Heal my wounds, God; I put my trust in you and know that you will see me through the storm. Amen.

DAY 18

All my plans will be fulfilled, for I know the end from the beginning.

Isaiah 46:10 (KJV)

SOMETIMES IT IS HARD TO ACCEPT THAT GOD IS IN CONTROL of every aspect of our lives. We can think we are mere puppets in His bigger story. But each of us has a role to play in His great plan. We all have an opportunity to be more like Jesus and to be His disciples, thus enabling us to live for Him. We have the privilege of serving others so they may come to know their Lord and saviour.

When have your plans ever worked out? Can you remember a time when God's plans were better than yours? As your dream died, God's plan took first place and you knew you were in perfect alignment with His plan for your life.

I have learnt over time that God and His plan are better for me than my own plans, although at times it is difficult to accept. Wanting to be in control of our own lives is part of being flawed and human. We would rather run our own lives than trust God who has the best plan for us. We fight that, because yes, in one sense God gave us free will. But God also doesn't want us to be sad or hurt. He hates His children to be hurt. So, when we follow our own ways, we can often hurt ourselves because we don't listen to what God desires for us.

Learn to tune in to God, to be on the same wavelength with Him. God gives us desires and hopes. Delight yourself in the Lord and He will give you the desires of your heart. Pursue those. But we need to seek wise counsel, and to spend a lot of time in prayer and reading the word of God to be able to discern between our own plans and God's will for our lives.

Usually, when you have a sense of settled peace about a situation, it means that it is God's will. Also, when you are experiencing true joy and feel completely whole, then you know that you are doing God's will.

Have you ever experienced times when you felt that peace? And knew you were exactly where God wanted you to be? If so, can you remember how you felt?

Prayer Starter

Dear Lord, please help me to accept your plans for my life and not my own. Amen.

DAY 19

Now faith is being sure of what we hope for and certain of
what we do not see.

Hebrews 11:1 (NIV)

DO WE TAKE STEPS OF FAITH DESPITE FEAR, REFUSING FEAR'S control? People often say that we take a leap of faith by believing in something we do not see. Faith and fear cannot co-exist. 'Lord, I believe. Help me in my unbelief.'

Faith is the absolute belief that God is working behind every scene in our lives even if there is no tangible evidence to support this fact.

Fear is the opposite of faith. It is unbelief or weak belief. This means that when fear/unbelief takes the upper hand it can take our emotions hostage.

Christian faith is the confident assurance of knowing that God loves me, God loves you, God loves us. And the only way for this faith to grow is by trusting Father God and by reading the Bible daily. We need spiritual food to grow in the same way that our body needs food to be nourished.

Would it be easier to live with fear or to live by faith? After all, you do not see fear. You do not see your future and yet you fear it. I think living by fear is much harder than living by faith. When you live by fear, you have a constant negative humdrum in your head, thinking of all the what-if-this-goes-wrongs, and all the whys. In some ways it is easier to live by fear, because we are humans living in a fallen world and we don't always want to believe that Father loves us and that He will really make everything alright.

Both motivating influences – fear and faith – are invisible. Why, then, is it harder to live with fear than to live by faith? What is it that draws us to live by fear more than by taking a knowing step of faith?

Prayer Starter

Dear Lord, please help me to live by faith and let me abandon a life of fear. Fear has no place in my heart. Help me to believe that you know what is best for me, and to know that, even if we don't know our futures, what you have in store for us is what is best. Amen.

Dark Night of the Soul

My fleeing soul is panic-stricken
In the darkness of the night,
Fused to a life of intimidating fear,
Not understanding the whys and what-ifs
Of all that has occurred.
Life, life, life rolling in one
Asymmetrical line of self-doubt and uncertainty,
Wondering the marvels of heavens above:
What is the purpose of this life?
Hurt and comfort merged together,
Wounded I stumble to the Cross
Where the soothing crème
Heals the deep assaults of pain
On my bitter soul of grief.
Curled up like a tiny foetus
On my bed
I rock back and forth
Silently crying for all that
Could have been but
Isn't to be.
My soul in the darkness of the night
Knows not of all that has occurred,
But as dawn rises
The assault of pain, panic diminishes once more
And I am set free by the power of the Cross;
My saviour has come once more for me
And showered His love upon me,
Immeasurably more.

DAY 20

Be joyful in hope, patient in affliction, faithful in prayer.

Romans 12:12 (NIV)

USUALLY, WHEN WE ARE STRUGGLING WE TEND TO FEED ourselves with negative thought processes. We tend to look for the bad in a situation rather than the good. We tend to wallow in self-pity and succumb to the devil's snare. But really what we should be doing is faithfully praying while we go through those periods of darkness.

We need to have a good and godly attitude towards the trials and tribulations of life. Joy is different from happiness. Happiness is a mood, but real joy in the Lord is much deeper.

Joy comes from having the assurance that whatever happens in our lives, God is in control. Even when going through a trial, it is the assurance of knowing that God knows what He is doing and will look after each one of our needs. It is about having peace in the current situation, even if we don't like the situation. It is about accepting it, rather than fleeing from it.

> *I am not saying this because I am in need, for I have learned to be content whatever the circumstances. I know what it is to be in need, and I know what it is to have plenty. I have learned the secret of being content in any and every situation, whether well fed or hungry, whether living in plenty or in want. I can do all this through him who gives me strength.*

> *Philippians 4:11-13 (NIV)*

This Bible verse is so important to me, as it teaches us to accept every situation. We know that our Father is in control. Rather than keeping living in the constant turmoil of what will happen now, in uncertainty about the future, we should approach every situation with a relaxed attitude. We know that God will be right beside us whatever we are going through.

God is an amazing Father and He wants us to be satisfied and for us to trust Him. Yes, it can be tough, but at the end of the day it will be totally worth it. Hallelujah!

Prayer Starter

Dear Lord, please help me to be content in any and every situation. Let me trust you and believe that you are in control of every aspect of my life. I have every confidence that you will see me through whatever situation I am in, because you love me. Amen.

DAY 21

Your word is a lamp for my feet, a light on my path.

Psalm 119:105 (NIV)

AS I PONDER THIS BIBLE VERSE AND REFLECT ON THE LAST two-and-a-half years, I realise that the Lord is indeed the lighthouse of my life. He guides me where the safe channels are to avoid the rocks. He guides me on the right course.

Who is your lighthouse? Do you let God lead you or do you allow yourself to be led astray?

How can we let God be the guiding lamp of our lives? Do we need to let go of ourselves? Do we need to be more open to hear what God is telling us? Our daily lives are so cluttered with day-to-day junk, that we do not always take the time or energy to sit still in the Lord's presence.

When my little boy died, in a sense I had to be forced to sit in stillness. Often during a desert period, God uses those moments to draw us close to Him. It is usually a time of deep cleansing, a time when God refreshes our soul. He nourishes our broken souls till they are healed. When Sebby died, I could not cope with the noise and clutter of large social gatherings. I often found myself drifting towards silence, as I couldn't cope with laughter and the general noise of day-to-day life. I had to sit still before the Lord. In a way, I had to sit in front of His Cross so that I could nail each of my burdens onto it, ultimately learning to hear His voice again and to feel His healing power over my very broken soul.

God helped me to see a purpose in the tragedy. It didn't come right away, but with each day, as I pressed into Him and felt His loving arms around me, I knew that there was a God who comforted the hearts of broken people. I knew that He was guiding me to something better, even if that somehow didn't sound right. God gave me the words to voice my anguish and through those words He would speak to me and guide me. He would show me a way out of the sadness and how to be content with my situation, even if I didn't understand it.

Prayer Starter

Dear Lord, please let Your word guide me onto the path of righteousness. Light my path so that I may follow you and cling onto you, whether it is through the storm or through periods of calm. Thank you, Lord, for Your word – the word that guides my feet to everlasting life. Amen.

DAY 22

He heals the broken-hearted and binds up their wounds.

Psalm 147:3 (NIV)

GRIEF IS A COMPLEX RESPONSE IN THE FACE OF LOSS, PARticularly when it is the death of something/someone with whom a bond has been formed.

Grief affects all areas of life. From an emotional response to loss, it can also be manifested physically, cognitively, behaviourally, socially, culturally and philosophically.

Certain types of loss, such as a stillbirth, bring a multitude of emotions ranging from the loss of hope to despair, anxiety, loss of control or a feeling of failure. Added to that grief, behind those emotions that are masked, is the issue that stillbirth is still a taboo subject. No-one wants to talk about the loss of a baby within the womb because it brings out the emotions of failure. People feel ashamed that they were not able to keep their child alive. In my experience, we are frowned upon.

Others don't know how to express sympathy when someone loses a baby to stillbirth. It is a difficult experience for them to deal with. They don't know what to say.

Often when people grieve, they do so in an unconstructive way. I have often noticed that people tend to bury their grief and try to forget it. They don't want to remember it and prefer to move on quickly, to forget. They bury their grief, but later in life it becomes a festering ball of uncontrolled anger, despair, frustration and extreme sadness.

If you bury all these emotions wrapped around grief, you bury them alive. You may temporarily starve them of oxygen, but eventually they will build up, they will bubble up to the surface. They will rear their ugly heads and come to haunt you. Is it not better just to embrace grief and your pain, trusting that God will see you through? Yes, I know this pain can be all-consuming, and often it feels like you are being broken in half. But Father is there for you, ready for you to run into His waiting arms, so that He can love you and heal you.

Prayer Starter

Dear Lord, please help me to embrace grief. Please don't let me run away from it. Help me to deal with my grief in an effective way. Amen.

DAY 23

He wipes every tear from their eyes, and there will be no more death or sorrow or crying or pain. All these things are gone forever.

Revelation 21:4 (NIV)

TO GRIEVE IN A HEALTHY WAY, IT NEEDS TO BE CONSTRUCT-ive. A person needs to have an outlet. There are many ways to grieve constructively.

Some people write, others turn their grief into beautiful pieces of music[4] while others turn it into beautiful cascading paintings bursting with colour.

When my son died, I began to write a lot. I wrote poetry. I wrote reflective pieces. I ached. I walked. I read grief books. I listened to music. In the beginning, my writing had a lot of self-condemnation and emotional turmoil – it was a purging motion. It helped me to get rid of all the negative pent-up emotions inside my heart.

The best place to lay your grief and all those erupting emotions that overwhelm you is at the foot of the Cross. This is ultimately where true healing occurs. It is where one meets God in the most intimate of intimate ways and where you can pour out your emotions and in return feel the compassion of God. You purge yourself of that grief and pin it to the Cross. In return, Father God takes your burden and frees you. You feel lighter and more able to carry on with life.

Prayer Starter

Dear Lord, I pin each and every single erupting emotion on the Cross so that I can be healed by the stripes of Jesus. Amen.

---

[4] e.g. *Tears in Heaven* by Eric Clapton

DAY 24

I will cover you all day long as you rest between my shoulders.

Deuteronomy 33:12 (NIV)

WHERE DO YOU TAKE YOUR COMFORT FROM? DO YOU TAKE it from God? Or do you take it from the people around you? How does comfort from God differ from the comfort that people give? I used to crave comfort from people – I still do, sometimes – but now I realise that the best comfort comes from God, not from people. God is the only one who can fill that empty void inside you, not people. People can only help to a certain extent; the greatest comforter, the greatest healer is God. The God I know is a compassionate God, a gracious God, a God of grace, a God of mercy, a zealous God, a God who knows my every need, even when I don't always know what my real needs are.

God can fulfil my needs. He can give me peace. He can comfort me. I can rest in the shadow of His wings and know without a doubt that I am safe – safe in the arms of Jesus.

When Sebastian died, the best place for me was to rest in God's arms and know the love and peace that surpasses all understanding – knowing that God carries the brunt of my suffering, and that I am only carrying a small portion of it. God does not like to see His people suffer. He uses suffering to draw us close to Him, so that in turn we learn to rely on Him for everything and not just for the usual emergency crisis that happens from day to day.

Take your comfort in God. Rest in His arms. Get to know God. Get to know that God loves you. Develop a relationship with Him by getting to know God. Read His word. Pray to Him. Call on His name and He will answer you. Talk to Him.

Prayer Starter

Dear Father God, teach me more about you. Let me rest in your loving arms, please. Help me, Lord, as I seek cover under your wings. Amen.

DAY 25

I cared for you in the wilderness, in the land of drought.

Hosea 13:5 (NIV)

WHEN YOU GO THROUGH DEEP, ANGUISHED SUFFERING, IT IS like being in the desert or on a battlefield. I remember when my son died that I did not want to be with anyone. I couldn't cope with large social gatherings. I needed to be in a safe place, a haven, where I was not criticised for my emotions or feelings but could safely unload them and feel lighter. The haven was my sanctuary, the place where I met with God.

Have you ever experienced God's care for you as you journeyed through the desert? Even if we feel that God is a distant God, it is merely our perception. He is always very close to us and holds us up when we fall. He cares for us even when we can't feel His presence. When you reflect on those years gone by, you realise that by the grace of God you got through the storm. And the truth is, you didn't get through the storm in your own strength but by His. Hallelujah!

The desert is where God meets you and strips you bare to see if you will really trust Him or if you will turn your back on Him. It is important to remember that sometimes God uses this period to see where your heart is. Is it with people or is it with Him, knowing that He will gather you up in His arms and comfort you at the darkest point in the journey? God does not abandon His children. In fact, it grieves Him to see his people suffer and it brings Him joy when we run to Him for guidance and for comfort. When we surrender our struggles, we find the freedom that Father wants us to have.

We are never alone in the wilderness for Father is with us wherever we go.

Prayer Starter

Dear Lord, please help me to embrace the wilderness rather than run from it. Help me to focus on your love, and not the lies of the enemy. Help me to surrender my struggles so that I can be free. Amen.

DAY 26

Consider it pure joy, my brothers and sisters, whenever you face trials of many kinds, because you know that the testing of your faith produces perseverance.

James 1:2-3 (NIV)

WHEN WE GO THROUGH A TRIAL, WE SOMETIMES FEEL THAT God is against us. 'Why is God against me? Why is God punishing me?'

We can question God in times of deep turmoil. 'Why has God banished me to the wilderness?' God allows bad things to happen in this world and in our lives. He uses suffering to draw us close to Him. He strips us bare to find out what is in our hearts. Will it be anger towards Him? Or will it be praise and trust, like David in Psalm 63?

What is your approach to the wilderness? Do you praise the Lord and trust Him to get you through? Or do you curse God and rely on your own strength to get you through a difficult time? Can you rely on your own strength to get through it? And if so, where will that lead you? Will it lead you astray? Will you muddle on, not really knowing what way to go? Will you suffer more?

Over the years I have learnt that the sooner I trust the Lord in all situations, especially in a difficult one, the easier it will be for Him to meet me and to grant me peace and grace. If we seek God's presence, if we worship Him, praise Him and know that He is bigger than our problems, then I believe that we can get through the situation much more quickly. It always seems easier to take a shortcut. But the reality is that taking a shortcut can be messy; it can lead us astray and can bring a whole host of new issues to the fore. Be like the psalmist David. Trust the Lord. Exalt His Holy Name.

Prayer Starter

Dear Lord, help me to take the right path through the wilderness and not a shortcut. Help me to focus on you and the price at the end. Teach my spirit what you want me to know during this wilderness period. Amen.

DAY 27

He lifted me out of the pit of despair,
He has given me a new song to sing.
Oh the joy of those who trust in the Lord.

Psalm 40:2-4 (NIV)

IT IS OFTEN HARD TO IMAGINE HOW GOD CAN LIFT US OUT of the pit of despair, how He can bind up our broken wounds. But because of God's great love, He can heal wounds that no-one else can.

The Lord is close to the broken-hearted;
He rescues those whose spirits are crushed.

Psalm 34:18

When you are broken-hearted, what do you do to help yourself out of the pit of despair? How do you get out of that deep and painful place? How do you go from a place of deep despair to a place of peace and rest? Do you pray, sing, worship? Do you put your focus on yourself or someone far greater than your problems – someone who loves you unconditionally, no matter what?

After my son died, I spent a lot of time listening to music and reading books that could help me to understand the emotions I was going through. The right music can lift your mood or emotions, but Christian music can lift you up spiritually. However, you must remember that both are valid forms of therapy. There should be no obligation to listen to Christian music alone. You should also be able to listen to your favourite secular music, within reason. In fact, both types of music serve a purpose; people should not be condemned for listening to secular music. Some secular music can also help a person come to terms with their deep grief.

I often say music is very healing for the soul. A lot of music, whether secular or Christian, comes from a place where there is deep emotion that needs to be released. Many people can often relate to the songwriter's anguish because we have been there – maybe not on the same road, but a similar road.

If you can get to a place of peace and rest through it, then any kind of music has served its purpose. It has helped you find the comfort that you need, enough to give you strength to face a new day.

Prayer Starter

Dear Lord, please help me to find the right music that speaks to my soul. Help me to come to a place of deep peace and rest in your presence. In your presence is fullness of joy. Amen.

DAY 28

Blessed are those whose strength is in you, whose hearts are set on pilgrimage, as they pass through the valley of Baca, they make it a place of springs.

Psalm 84:5-6 (NIV)

WITHOUT WANTING TO SOUND OFFENSIVE, THERE IS A COR-rect way and an incorrect way to grieve. Over the past couple of years, I have seen that so many people grieve incorrectly – simply by ignoring their grief.

It pains me to see how so many people are hostage to grief. There are different types of grief, but you don't have to let it define you. You can let go of it and give it to God, so that you can be free.

Some people go into automatic mode when they are grieving. They go into a state where they want to forget that part of life like it never happened. The reality is that it did exist. In fact, by trying to forget it, they bury their grief and its emotions. The problem is in time it will rear its ugly head to the surface.

How do you overcome grief? How do you integrate the person who taught you so much about life back into your life? How do you honour their memory? At times, it can hurt so much.

But is it wise to forget that person, to bury them, to bury the feelings of deep anguish? If you bury those feelings alive, they will resurface one day. And then what? How do you face them when they resurface, as they inevitably will? Do you return to the endless cycle of denial and merely function?

Do you go onto an endless treadmill of what-ifs? The what-ifs can destroy you; they can cause so much unnecessary pain in your life, sometimes to the point that you can no longer function.

The Hebrew word 'baca' means 'to weep'. In scriptural terms going through the valley of Baca is a form of spiritual renewal, being refreshed and made new. You can pass through the valley of weeping or you can get stuck in it. If you come through the valley of weeping, it becomes a well-spring of life. If you don't pass through the valley of grief, you become hostage to grief, and it will destroy you and prevent you from becoming the person that God created you to be.

Prayer Starter

Dear Lord, please help me to go through the valley of Baca and make it a place of springs. Help me to face my grief and have the strength to overcome it. Help me to be the person you created me to be. Amen.

DAY 29

Do not be conformed to this world, but be transformed by
the renewal of your mind, that by testing you may discern
what is the will of God, what is good and acceptable and
perfect.

Romans 12:2 (NIV)

WHEN SEBASTIAN DIED, I HAD SO MANY DIFFERENT EMO-
tions that were completely tearing me apart – emotions that I could not
really understand. I questioned my very existence before God. I
questioned my purpose in life. If I weren't meant to be a mother, would
I ever be a mother? I felt like God was putting me to the test. I questioned
Him. 'What great sin have I committed that I have been banished to the
wilderness?'

I felt God was punishing me for some great past sin that I must have
committed. Life felt bitterly unfair. One friend was happily married and
welcomed her son at the end of the pregnancy. I was divorced and lost
everything. The sheer anguish of that reality was incomprehensible.
There were questions that raced around my head. I could choose to go
down the route of bitterness or I could choose to put my confidence in
God and believe that He had a plan for my life.

'Why me, God? Why me? What did I do wrong to deserve this? What
is your purpose in all of this?'

The truth is, God does not banish us to the wilderness. God wants
you to embrace it. He uses it to draw us near to Him so that we can learn
about His love towards us.

I had to learn to embrace the wilderness, rather than run from it. I
had to learn to accept that now I am in the wilderness and I must walk
through it or crawl through it. I must not run from it, because sooner or
later it will catch up with me and I will be flung back into it.

Prayer Starter

Dear Lord, help me to be at peace and not to be afraid of the wilderness. Teach me what you want to teach me. Help me to choose the path of righteousness and not the path of bitterness. Amen.

Can You Love Me?

Can you love me –
With all my faults:
Angst; fear of rejection, abandonment
That plagues my soul
And seems to drown me at times
In the thick slushy sand?

I lay my soul bare for you to see.
I lay it all down, the good and bad.
I show you where I am at:
A broken woman enslaved to sin
But saved by grace.
Can you really, truly love me
For who I am?

Can you love me
Unconditionally and see that I am
Trying to be at peace;
That I am trying to hold you up,
Encourage you, support you,
Whilst I prevent myself from
Falling, falling, falling
Into the pit of despair?

My hope is at the foot of the Cross,
My peace comes from God,
But I am a woman enslaved by sin
Striving to live a better life
Following the footsteps of Jesus.
Can you truly love me
For who I am?

Can you love me?
Can you see that I am trying to be still,
Trying to be silent?
Can you love me?
Can you really, truly love me?

Day 30

Blessed is the one who perseveres under trial because, having stood the test, that person will receive the crown of life that the Lord has promised to those who love him.

James 1:12 (NIV)

DURING TRIAL AND TRIBULATION GOD TEACHES US NOT TO compare our situation to other people's because that can lead to feelings that shouldn't be there such as: *jealousy; despair; insecurity; feeling like a failure; not being accomplished enough; not being worthy enough.*

Comparison can be the devil's trap. And what good does it bring to us? Does it bring our children back? Our lost dreams? Our plans that we had? Does it bring back what we have lost? No. It just leads to an unceasing circle of negativity.

I had to change my mindset and not compare my situation to other people's, because it just brought me down. I had to see the positive from my situation. I had to think:

- What can I learn from this experience?
- What can I learn during this deeply painful period in my life?
- Can I learn to replace the lies of the devil with truths of God?
- Can I learn something and then pass it on to some other poor soul in the same boat as me?

I decided to use the wilderness period as a time to listen to what God wanted to teach me, so that one day I could pass it on to people. I decided it was more important to learn from it than to wallow in self-pity. So, I embarked on a journey of self-discovery, of learning who I was but also who God was.

In the same way, you too can change your perspective on trials and tribulation and see what God has to teach you. Learn something from it so that you can pass it on to the next person. Use it to your benefit so that when you enter a new trial, you know how to apply what you learnt to the new situation. Don't be afraid of silence. Let God work in you so that you can experience the peace that He wants His children to experience.

Prayer Starter

Dear Lord, please give me a teachable spirit, and a spirit to discern what you want to teach me. Help me to use those principles to help myself and others. Amen.

DAY 31

...a voice of one crying in the wilderness, 'Make ready the way of the Lord, make his paths straight.'

Mark 1:3 (NIV)

ONCE YOU LEARN TO ACCEPT THE WILDERNESS, YOU WILL then see gradual progress in your life. However, be warned, it won't just happen overnight. It will take time. Healing will occur as God teaches you how to cope with the onslaught of negative emotions. Healing will occur as you surrender each one of your struggles at the foot of the Cross and when you learn to forgive yourself. God teaches you about trusting Him again in each and every situation.

It becomes a lesson of acceptance. It becomes a time of deep spiritual healing; a time when you become completely whole again, if you allow God to cleanse you from the inside out with the cleansing blood of Jesus.

Challenging times should be regarded as a blessing rather than condemnation. Instead of feeling self-pity for yourself when you are going through a trial, confront your fearful emotions. Tell your negative emotions that they have no place in your life. Replace the negativity with positive affirmations from God.

Trust God. Live by faith. Don't run a hundred miles in the opposite direction when confronted with pain but welcome it and work through it. Work through it with godly counsellors. Spend time with the Lord.

In his song, *The Table,* Chris Tomlin says that God invites us to come to His table just as we are, and we can then experience healing. Pour out your emotions. It is better for them to come out than to stay inside. Do not be afraid to unveil yourself at the foot of the Cross. The whole point of the wilderness experience is to bring spiritual maturity into your life, and to help you become the person that God wants you to be.

Prayer Starter

Dear Lord, I have confidence in you to see me through this wilderness period. Help me to replace the lies of the enemy with positive affirmations. Help me, Lord, to seek your presence. Amen.

DAY 32

*But they [the Israelites] soon forgot what he had done and
did not wait for his plan to unfold. In the desert, they gave in
to their craving; in the wilderness, they put God to the test.*

Psalm 106:13-14 (NIV)

LEARNING TO RECOGNISE WHEN YOU GO INTO DENIAL CAN
help you avoid it. We are wired for pleasure and not for pain. But when
we are in pain, we should listen to that pain. It is trying to tell us
something. We need to have an open mind and ask what it is
communicating.

Pain is a warning sign, often when something is wrong, whether we
are physically sick or emotionally broken. It can be helpful when it is
graciously recognised as an instrument to form a compassionate
character. If we never had any challenges in our lives, how are we to be
empathetic to other people who are traveling the same road of grief as
we are?

Basically, we need to go head-on into pain to overcome that place of
deep anguish. The fact is, no-one likes to suffer. No-one likes to face the
pain head-on. If we had a chance we would avoid it or skirt around it.
But with the help of Father God we can face whatever tribulation we are
facing.

Trusting God is key to overcoming pain. Embracing pain is key to
overcoming pain. Sitting at the foot of the Cross is key to overcoming
pain. The Cross doesn't necessarily have to be a physical cross in a
church. It just means spending an hour a day or more with God and
giving your clenched emotions to Him, our Father. It means talking to
Him and giving your struggles to Jesus. He died for you and your
struggles, so that you can be free. Hallelujah!

Prayer Starter

*Dear Lord, help me to recognise denial so that I can avoid it. Help me to
understand my pain and learn to release it so that I can be free. Help me*

to focus on the positive in my life and to share my pain with you. Help me to talk to you. Speak to my broken heart, I pray. Amen.

DAY 33

Then Jesus said to His disciples, 'If anyone wishes to come after Me, he must deny himself, and take up his Cross and follow me. For whoever wishes to save his life will lose it, but whoever loses his life for My sake will find it.'

Matthew 16:24-25 (NIV)

ONCE YOU SURRENDER YOUR STRUGGLES TO FATHER, YOU will experience the deep healing that He wants you to experience. But you have to be open for it, you have to be ready to change. It is about surrendering to the will of God and learning to accept. Once you embrace this pain, and once you establish a good daily routine of worshipping and talking, praying to God, healing will occur. Remember though, it won't happen overnight. But God will heal your wounds.

If you avoid pain and bury it, you bury it alive and it will resurface in later years through a crisis in your life. I found that it is better to embrace pain with zeal, joy and peace, and to accept it, rather than try to push it away. Don't enter a warzone with it, because ultimately unresolved pain can make you a prisoner to it. This in turn leads you to having a wounded spirit.

Surrender your struggles to the Lord.

Prayer Starter

Dear Lord, thank you for your love and compassion towards me. Thank you for your grace. Lord, help me to embrace pain; help me to surrender my struggles to you, so that I do not have to face them alone. Thank you, Lord, for restoring my soul. Thank you, Lord. Amen.

DAY 34

Train up a child in the way he should go,
even when he is old he will not depart from it.

Proverbs 22:6 (NIV)

OUR UPBRINGING INFLUENCES HOW WE REACT TO SITUA-
tions in our lives. It means that when we go through difficult times we
may not know how to react to the onslaught of emotions.

Our upbringing can set the tone of our response to trials and
tribulations, whether in a positive or negative manner. If you have never
seen your parents fight or argue, you may not know how to respond to
conflict, and feel that you are thrown into the middle of a wilderness
when you yourself are faced with it.

Some people grew up suppressing their emotions because they were
taught not to express them but rather to ignore their volcanic eruption.
It is a very common problem.

People tend to avoid the rawness of emotions because it scares them.
Avoidance is the wrong way to respond to trials. Yes, you may be afraid
of your emotions, but if you insist on avoiding them, how will you find
healing in your life? How will you overcome pain? How will you get
through the confusion if you don't face these issues head-on?

Many of us have grown up with the belief that expressing our
emotions is a sign of weakness. Clearly, this is not a sign of weakness,
but a sign of resilience and courage in the face of adversity – a sign of
strength of character. Why should we be ashamed of our emotions? Why
should we have to bury them alive?

God gave us emotions so that we can express them, provided that we
do it in the right way; provided that we don't fall into a trap of self-pity,
but work through them in a constructive, healing and restorative way.
God will free us and enable us to use our emotions to connect with others
who have travelled a similar road to us.

Prayer Starter

Dear Lord, please help me to face trials and tribulations with strength of character, rather than suppressing all the negative emotions. Show me, Lord, I pray. Amen.

DAY 35

'I have told you these things, so that in me you may have peace. In this world you will have trouble. But take heart! I have overcome the world.'

John 16:33 (NIV)

TO HAVE A GODLY ATTITUDE IN THE FACE OF TRIALS IS paramount in overcoming the tribulations in your life. It is not an easy lesson to learn. But it is a fundamental factor in your healing journey.

The devil wants you to sit around feeling sorry for yourself, wallowing in your own misery and feeding on lies that say you are incapable of getting over it. People want you to get over it quickly and move on. People don't want you to talk about your problems.

But if you feel as though you are sinking into the pits of despair, my advice is to read Psalm 63 aloud every day until the depression lifts. This can be your prayer, your antidepressant and your rescue remedy.

The first thing I remember doing after my son died was praying, worshipping and singing to my Lord. It was a slow journey to recovery. But I made it a basic principle of my healing journey to cling onto the faith that I had learnt throughout my pregnancy and the years before that.

I had to learn not to talk negatively to myself. This is easier said than done. It is still a steep learning curve for me to make positive affirmations to myself rather than to talk negatively. I am learning to replace the lies with truths from the Bible.

Don't let people bully you into having to get over this trial quickly. The wilderness experience will take as long as it takes. We should not have to be ashamed of being in the wilderness as we let God help us deal with things.

Being in the *wilderness* is not a weakness. It is a *strength*. It should be *embraced* with zeal and peace. It is a place where deep spiritual healing can occur, if you let God work through you. It is a place where you can find rest under the protective wings of God. It is a place where you can learn about God's unfailing love for us. Embrace it and be *free*.

Prayer Starter

Dear Father God, your strength is my strength. I worship you. I sing you praises for you are a great, big God and you are in control of my life. Help me to face my struggles with a godly attitude and not a negative one. I want to be free in your name. Amen.

Day 36

A generous person will prosper, whoever refreshes others will be refreshed.

Proverbs 11:25 (NIV)

GRIEF'S JOURNEY INVOLVES TAKING A STEP OF COURAGE SO that we can move forward past our pain. It was courage that taught me to face my fears, and it was courage that taught me to move forward into the unknown. Faith is an act of courage to trust God that He will get us through the painful wilderness of deep human anguish. Yet when fear hits, and you realise that your issues are overwhelming you, how do you get the strength to keep going? How do you keep moving forward?

God gives us courage to face the trials of life that are staring us in the face. It is faith that helps us see that there is hope and that there is light at the end of a dark tunnel. But to move forward from grief, you must be *willing* to see the endless possibilities that surround you, rather than let the negative consume you. Grief does not need to define who you are. Grief fuels the courage within you that will enable you to move forward. Courage laughs in the face of fear, so that you do not have to be hostage to grief for the rest of your life. God does not want you to be a hostage. Our Father God wants you to be at peace. He wants you to have a future without grief holding you back. He wants you to unveil yourself at the foot of the Cross and to release your burdens. Only then can you move forward without forgetting who you are and what happened to you.

There is no shame in your past. Your past can define you, but it doesn't have to be set in concrete. Only your past can merge you with the new you; this is a far better alternative. If you learn to accept that, you will be free.

It is courage that helps you to choose life over death, the path of light rather than the path of darkness. It is courage that leads you to the Cross, where you surrender yourself to God and receive healing from the inside out from Him. Courage is taking a step of faith, believing that He is walking beside you, while also knowing with confident assurance that He has a plan for your life.

Sometimes courage is the quiet voice at the end of the day saying, 'I'll try again tomorrow.'

Prayer Starter

Dear Father God, please give me the courage to face my grief journey today. Please give me the strength to face the grief journey. Please take away any shame inside of me. Amen.

DAY 37

In all things God works for the good of those who love him.

Romans 8:28 (NIV)

JESUS COMFORTS ME DURING MY TRIALS AND TRIBULA-
tions. He collects my tears and puts them quietly in little bottles marked
'Hannah's Grief'.

Grief is a long, difficult and often painful journey. You frequently
don't know what will happen on this road or where it may lead you. It
takes courage to want to change your attitude and to stop thinking, 'Why
me?' Sometimes there does not need to be a reason why things happen;
sometimes we just have to accept it. It is a hard lesson to learn, but maybe
a lesson worth knowing.

I know from personal experience that if you take a step away from
the spotlight and learn to focus on the Cross rather than your own hurts,
life will suddenly make a whole lot more sense. It is hard to put into
practice. But when you do learn to focus on the bigger picture, you get
remarkable results.

In my life, when I hit a rough patch after the storm, my eyes began to
focus on the Cross and what it means for me. The Cross is where I lay
my burdens down and it is where I have to give up my son so that he may
have a better life than all the suffering that we face daily on the earth.
You learn to seek meaning in life when everything has gone pear-shaped.

It is about learning to forgive yourself, about letting go of the pain,
the guilt, the fear, the hopelessness, and learning to believe that there is
hope and that there is light at the end of the dark, long tunnel. It was
about learning to see through a looking-glass that clearly focuses on the
present rather than the past, and not through the rose-tinted looking-
glass that focuses on a dream-like state, a reality that no longer exists.
Let go. Let God. Be free in the image of Christ.

Prayer Starter

*Dear Lord, please help me to rest in you when everything isn't going the
way I planned it. Help me to trust that your plans are best for me. Help*

me to surrender my struggles at the Cross so that I can be free. It is through you that I can be healed. Fill me with your peace, I pray. Heal me, please. Amen.

DAY 38

May the God of hope fill you with all joy and peace as you
trust in Him, so that you may overflow with hope by the
power of the Holy Spirit.

Romans 15:13 (NIV)

CAN WE LAUGH, HAVE A SENSE OF HUMOUR AND HAVE JOY even during a heavy trial? Or should it all be gloom and doom? Should we be sad all the time? I think Father blesses us with laughter, a sense of humour and joy even when the going gets tough. Laughter and a sense of humour can be a release from all the heavy emotions that surround us day in, day out.

I remember the first time I laughed after Sebastian died. I froze. I was paralysed in fear. It felt like a betrayal to my son's life. It felt odd to my ears. I was deranged by guilt. I felt like I was dishonouring my son's memory – like I didn't love him enough. The truth was, I needed a break from the intensity in my life. I believe a sense of humour, laughter and joy are blessings and gifts from God our Father to relieve us of overwhelming, disempowering emotions that seem impossible to escape.

Job said that if we pray and remember the blessings of Father God, He will restore our joy and righteousness.[5] Even though we are suffering, God brings healing to us. Even if we walk in the barren desert, we will see flowers growing, and that brings hope. Such hope shows perseverance despite the shattering heart, the lack of meaning to life, after all else seems to have disappeared into the sands.

Have peace, for God gives and takes away. If we seek God's presence, if we remember that Father God is greater than our problems, and learn to worship Him in the barren desert, and learn to praise Him, only then can we experience healing, true joy and peace. Our hope is simply in Him, in the Cross. Our joy is not found in the material things in this world, but in Jesus who died for our sins. Only in Him may we have eternal life.

---

[5] See Job 33:26

Our joy comes from knowing that God is far greater than any trial/adversity we face.

Prayer Starter

Dear Lord, please fill me up with a hope that is unseen – a confident assurance that it is well with my soul even in the barren desert. Amen.

DAY 39

Then he said to them all: 'Whoever wants to be my disciple must deny themselves and take up their Cross daily and follow me.'

Luke 9:23 (NIV)

SOMETIMES I FIND MYSELF LOOKING AT THE SKY AND QUEST-ioning God. 'What is my purpose, God? What is the purpose of my life? What is the point?'

I ask. I question. I contemplate. I wonder.

It seems that the good moments in life are just like a fleeting bird, while the trials of life seem to lie heavily on one's heart.

There are two ways that one can approach life's trials and tribulations:

- approach them with zeal and faith;
- abandon faith.

Which is the better option? I know through experience that to approach life with zeal and faith is the better of the two. I also know that God will carry us through each trial we face. We must just call unto Him, and He will hear our cry and come to our rescue.

Some days I feel like I am just existing. Breathing. Getting through the day, only to go through the same mundane emotions again the following day. If I find that to be a trial, I pray like this:

Prayer Starter

Lord, help me to seek your will clearly, please, for my life. Help me to be faithful to you. Show me your way. I do not want to be a doormat. I want to move forward in life. Lord, help me to overcome the fear of rejection and the fear of abandonment. Help me to overcome the spirit of bitterness and help me to overcome my wounded spirit. Help me to be whole within you. You are my God. Hallelujah! I praise your Holy Name. Amen.

Abba, Abba, Do You Hear Me?

Abba, Abba, do you hear me, I need you
When my spirit is dry and broken.
Abba, break the chains
Of pain that bind me and keep
Me enslaved to sin.
I am lost in a world of brokenness
Where hope has left behind a mark.

Come find me, Abba.
Abba, Abba, I cry, come find me.
Come hold me, Abba, come hold me.
Abba, Abba do you hear my cries?

Abba, Abba, do you hear me, I am your daughter,
Enslaved to sin; forgive me, Abba,
Fill me with your everlasting hope.
Abba, I am filled with this terror
That plagues me by night and day.
Abba, hear my cry, hear my pleas.
Abba, hold me, please.

Come find me, Abba,
Abba, Abba, I cry, come find me.
Come hold me, Abba, come hold me.
Abba, Abba, do you hear my cries?

Abba, Abba, do you hear me, do you care about me
In a world where no-one seems to care
With the hustle and bustle of day-to-day life,
Trains to catch, flights to catch, morning rush hour traffic?
Abba, you are my Father, please love me.
Please do not forsake me,
Please do not leave me.

Come find me, Abba,
Abba, Abba, I cry, come find me.
Come hold me, Abba, come hold me.
Abba, Abba, do you hear my cries?

And Abba responds and says,
'Do not be afraid, my beloved child.
All is well. I am here for you.
I bear your pain and I give you
My peace.

Beloved child, I will show the way.
Do not be afraid.
Hear my soft voice;
I will always be here,
I will not go anywhere.
So my child, do not be afraid
For I am in control
And I love you.'

DAY 40

*Those who suffer he delivers in their suffering; he speaks to
them in their affliction.*

Job 36:15 (NIV)

GOD USES SUFFERING TO DRAW US NEAR TO HIM. SIN EN-
tered the world at the time of Adam and Eve – the time of the Fall.
Through suffering we become strong, we gain experience and we learn
to cope with what entered our world. In time, it allows us to help others
walking the path that we have already trodden ourselves.

God does not leave us here to suffer pointlessly. He has a perfect plan
to use that suffering to accomplish His purposes. He uses pain and
suffering to draw us to Himself, so that we will cling to Him. Jesus said,
'In the world, you shall have tribulation.'[6]

Suffering, tribulation and challenges are a part of life. It is part of
what it means to be human in a fallen world. But because we have God
in our lives, Christ is our anchor that holds fast in our storms. However,
if we do not sail into the centre of the storm, how will we know that our
Father is a gracious God, a Father of compassion, a God who bears the
brunt of our suffering? How do we know that unless we face our trials
head on with zeal and joy? It is only in times of our deepest distress and
sorrow that we reach out to Him, when all else has failed. It often takes
a crisis for us to turn to Him for help. What do we find? God is constant.
God never changes from the north to the south, from the east to the west.
When we reach out to God, he is waiting to comfort us and to uphold us
through it all. In this way, He proves His faithfulness to us and ensures
we will remain close to Him.

The question you have to ask yourself is, *will you sail straight into
the face of the storm, full steam ahead, or will you skirt around it? Will
you confront your need and experience healing from our Lord and
Saviour?*

When my son died, I decided that rather than facing this journey on
my own, I would cling to Father God. I decided to find courage to face

---

[6] See John 16:33

what was to be one of the most difficult times in my life. But I came through because I had God by my side every step of the way.

I want to encourage you, whatever you are facing, whether it is deep grief or relentless depression, to sail straight into the face and eye of the storm. Don't run away from it. In the long haul, it will be easier to enter the storm, because as you face the storm, the light will meet you. You will receive renewed hope and strength, and you will see God our Father's love for you.

Prayer Starter

Dear Father God, let me not face the storm alone but be with me wherever I go. Teach me your ways. Don't let me run away from grief. Teach me what you want me to learn. Strengthen me, oh Father God. Amen.

DAY 41

He lifted me out of the pit of despair, He has given me a new song to sing. Oh, the joy of those who trust the Lord.

Psalm 40:2-4 (NIV)

IT IS OFTEN HARD TO ACCEPT A DEVASTATING LOSS IN OUR lives. We often lose track of where God wants us to go, or we struggle to figure out the purpose of what our lives are meant to be. What does God want me to do with my life? During turbulent times, it becomes hard to hear God's voice, or even to be *open* to His voice.

Even if He doesn't feel close, He is near to all. He knows every nuance of our emotions. But when the pain of brokenness is louder and creating upheaval in our lives, it becomes difficult to discern His soft voice.

This is when we need to learn to spend time in the Lord's presence by reading His word, praying to Him and worshipping Him. We do not need to be afraid or ashamed of sharing our raw emotions. This is hard to do because most people in our society today are afraid to express their emotions for fear of being perceived as weak. They are unable to cope with what life has thrown at us.

The Lord provides us with a safe place where we can unmask ourselves and let our emotions run raw – a place where we can be ourselves and experience the loving, healing touch of our Lord. This place is called the sanctuary. It can be at the foot of your bed, or at a physical cross in a church, or holding a small cross in your hand. But wherever you are, God is there too.

Prayer Starter

Dear Lord, thank you for your love and compassion. Help me to draw near to you; help me to hear your voice as the brokenness in my life is louder than anything else. Cleanse me from the inside out; purify my heart, oh Lord, I pray. Guide me. Heal me, Lord, teach me to be free. Amen.

DAY 42

Now we see through a glass darkly, but then ... face to face.

1 Corinthians 13:12 (NIV)

WE ALL WEAR MASKS. SOME HELP US TO GET THROUGH THE day in one piece and are relatively harmless, but others are unhealthy, particularly if they represent years of denial or anger regarding unresolved issues.

There are many different types of masks. The most common are:

- 'I am a success' mask.
- 'Everything's OK' mask.
- 'I never show emotions' mask.
- 'Tough guy' mask.
- 'Helpless female' mask.
- 'Hide the real me' mask.
- 'I am always happy' mask.
- 'Everything's wonderful and amazing' mask.
- 'Courting' mask.
- 'Grief' mask.

When my son died, I put on a mask of grief. But I also wore a 'hide the real me' mask. It was to avoid being weak (a form of denial), and to avoid people seeing the real turmoil inside of me, the simple anguish of losing my son to stillbirth. I wore an 'I am strong' mask to avoid being weak, but also simply to keep getting through the day. Was it bad to wear a mask?

In a sense, no, because it helped me to keep going. It helped me to keep crawling forward when all I wanted to do was to die. So, yes, sometimes wearing a mask can be a blessing in disguise.

But it is also important to remember that we should not have to wear a mask because we are embarrassed by our emotions. We should not have to be ashamed of our weaknesses or our imperfections. As believers we are all forgiven sinners needing help to be more like Jesus every day. We all have imperfections and it is by the grace of God that we can overcome anything.

Unmasking ourselves at the foot of the Cross is the key. It is a place where we can bare our raw emotions and nail all our struggles to the Cross. It is a place where we can be completely honest with ourselves and where we do not need to experience shame, but the love and compassion of God. Do not be afraid to uncover yourself at the foot of the Cross. This is where healing can occur, if you allow yourself to reveal your real self.

Prayer Starter

Dear Lord, help me to uncover my hidden emotions and hidden struggles and pin them to the Cross so that I can be free. Cleanse me from the inside out; purify me, Lord. Reveal yourself to me, I pray. Amen.

DAY 43

Surrender your heart to God, turn to Him in prayer.

Job 11:13 (NIV)

SURRENDERING TO GOD'S WILL IS A KEY PRINCIPLE TO accepting your loss. It helps to bring healing to your broken heart. It helps to bring closure and acceptance that God has the best plan for us. God's good plan always prevails, even if we want so badly to wake up earlier from this terrible nightmare. The sooner we come to accept our loss and to surrender to God's will, the easier the healing journey will be. This is easier said than done though.

It took me some time to put this principle into practice. It was hard to truly believe that God knew what was best for me. Every day I had to consciously give Sebastian to the Lord. I would pray this simple prayer:

'Dear Lord, I give you Sebastian and believe that you have a plan for me. Help me to let go of Sebastian without forgetting him. Lord, help me to accept this devastating loss. Help me to move forward with grace, love and compassion. Thank you for helping me to come to terms with my loss. Amen.'

Some days it was easier to give Sebastian to God than other days. Sometimes I just wanted to cling onto what once was but was not now to be. I was so angry that motherhood had been taken away from me. I am still a mother but not the mother of a living, breathing child.

'For I know the plans I have for you,' declares the Lord,
'plans to prosper you and not to harm you, plans to give you
hope and a future.'

Jeremiah 29:11

God has a plan for each of us. He gives and takes away. But that doesn't mean that He doesn't love us when He takes something away from us. God wants us to come to Him, whether the going is tough or easy. God wants us to call on Him and He will restore us at His table. He can give us peace, if we learn to trust that His perfect plan is the best for us, rather than our own plans which we tend to believe are better for us.

If I learnt anything in the last years since my son's passing, it is this: God can turn tragedy into something beautiful and that gives me hope. My hope is in God. And I will cling onto God in the good and bad times. God is my hope. He is my hope for my salvation, and He gives me great peace.

Prayer Starter

Dear Lord, I give you _____ and believe that you have a plan for me. Help me to let go of _____ without forgetting him/her. Lord, help me to accept this devastating loss. Help me to move forward with grace, love and compassion. Thank you for helping me to come to terms with my loss. Amen.

DAY 44

*So do not fear, for I am with you; do not be dismayed, for I
am your God. I will strengthen you and help you; I will
uphold you with my righteous right hand.*

Isaiah 41:10 (NIV)

THE UNKNOWN CAN BE A SCARY PLACE. FEAR AND ANXIETY
can hold you prisoner if you are not careful. When my son died, I feared
what the future was holding. Suddenly, here I was childless with my
hopes and dreams crashing down after the stillbirth, and I had to come
to terms with giving birth to a dead child. It all seemed impossible.

But the Lord was there with me in that hospital room of a communist
past. He strengthened me through His music to get through the birth and
to confront death head-on. This was one of the first times when I felt
death was confronting me and I was afraid of death. When I miscarried
my first two children, death did not have such a strong hold of me. When
Sebastian died, however, death challenged me and made me acutely
aware of how fragile life is.

Within a split second your life can change forever, and what was
meant to be is no more. The 'what-was-to-be' is snatched away, replaced
by shifting sands of time and a new normal appears from nowhere.

I was fearful of death; fearful of giving birth, fearful of what lay ahead
of me. Thick deep forests of grief awaited me. And I had a choice. Life
and Death were talking to me. To which voice would I listen? Would I
listen to Death's soft voice lulling me into a false sense of security? Or
would I listen to Life's harsh voice and choose to live? I was acutely aware
of my own existence and how fragile my life was. I was very ill at that
stage and I knew that I would die too.

But from out of nowhere strength and grace met, and made me tackle
death head-on; they made me face the birth of my son, but also face the
long, silent paths of grief. This strength was God. God saw me at my
toughest time. He carried me through the storm. He was present in that
hospital room as I was prepared to give birth to my son, and as I faced
death in new ways. Death was real. And it was not something to be afraid

of. Even if it bullied its way into my life. God was stronger. God's peace was stronger. God's love was stronger.

Am I afraid of death now? No – although, I do struggle with situations in which I have no control. That causes me stress. In such situations I know I must simply trust the Lord to see me through. In the same way, I want to encourage you to focus on the Lord whatever you are going through. God will carry you. You will not be alone.

Prayer Starter

Dear Father God, you are my God and I am not afraid for you are in control of everything. In you I place my trust. In you I seek refuge. I look up to you. Amen.

DAY 45

*And pray in the Spirt on all occasions with all kinds of
prayers and requests. With this in mind, be alert and always
keep on praying for all the Lord's people.*

Ephesians 6:18 (NIV)

A KEY TO GETTING THROUGH THE WILDERNESS IS YOUR prayer life. Prayer opens the communication channel between yourself and God – an honest and open relationship. It is also a unique experience in which you can experience God's love, compassion and wisdom. Let His words infuse into you.

I used to think that I should not be praying to God – what right did I have? When I was a little girl I would pray, but I struggled to hear the *rhema* word (the still, small voice). My spirit was not tuned into God's voice.

When you don't read the Bible or build up a relationship with God, how will you be able to hear the *rhema* word? God speaks to us everywhere. We just have to learn to tune into the word. Don't give up on your spiritual life, even if the going is tough. God loves to hear from His children. He loves it when we seek His presence and seek to know him more on a deeper level.

If you were to see God, what would you tell Him? What would you talk to Him about? Imagine that He is like a good friend, a Father. He understands everything and wants us to have freedom in Christ.

Prayer Starter

Dear Lord, please help me to hear your still, small voice. Help me to understand your word as I read the Bible, and help me to understand my grief, and to let it go and let you in. Amen.

DAY 46

The power of life and death is in the tongue/mouth.

Proverbs 18:21 (NIV)

IT IS EASY TO SUCCUMB TO NEGATIVITY AND SPEAK OF death rather than life over our souls when we experience deep, traumatic things. It is still easier to avoid pain. We want to die in the face of hostile pain.

But what does the Bible teach us? Certainly, if we keep speaking of death over ourselves, we will go into a negative spiral of self-pity, regret, sorrow and into a bottomless pit of deep depression. On the other hand, we can keep speaking life over ourselves with positive affirmation from the Bible. If we choose to do this, we feel the Lord's presence, peace and joy.

I remember a friend telling me to choose life over death. I spoke so negatively about myself that this became a welcome stronghold for the devil. He could persuade me to build on my insecurities such as feeling like a failure, not being good enough and being a bad mum to my son. The list goes on.

I had to confront these negative phrases and replace these negative thought processes with positive affirmations and truths from the Bible. I had to start believing that I was not a failure, but that I was able to succeed by the grace of God. I had to affirm that He would help me to overcome adversity. God helps us to focus on the good and not on the bad as we know that He is love.

It was a long, slow journey of affirmation over me, but it was worth it in the end. I want to encourage you: just because you are going through a difficult time and you're feeling useless and blaming yourself that it is your fault (even though it isn't), listen up – *it is not your fault.* You are a daughter/son of the King and God does not expect perfection. He does want us to go to Him with our troubles, so that He can help us to face them and learn to see ourselves in the light of Christ.

Prayer Starter

Dear Lord, please help me to speak life over my life and not death. Help me to speak the truths over myself. Help me to know your love for me. Amen.

DAY 47

God will direct your steps.

Proverbs 3:6 (NIV)

DO YOU BELIEVE THAT GOD CAN DIRECT YOUR STEPS? THAT He knows what is best for you? God says, 'I have plans for you... I know everything.'

Learn to trust our Father God. Each time we face trials we begin to doubt that God can see us through this pain, but He never fails, He always helps us regardless. Do we want to live life on a rollercoaster, having moments of doubt and moments of faith? Or do we want that deep assurance of knowing that God will see us through, no matter what?

Often, we think that our plans are better than what God has in store for us. But over the years, I have gradually come to realise that God's plans are better than my plans, and that He will direct my steps if I am obedient to the Holy Spirit. If I allow myself to tune in to the Holy Spirit, I will know what the Lord wants me to do.

After Sebastian died, I was unsure of what to do. Suddenly, everything that was mapped out for me was taken away, and I had no map to navigate through the abyss. I had no map telling me what lay ahead. Motherhood was suddenly stolen from me and I felt very alone.

I had no strength of my own. I had to believe that God would direct my steps (somehow); that God would guide me through the wilderness to the other side. I needed to remain obedient to Him and stay in tune with the Holy Spirit. God would then guide me to a place of safety.

In the same way God can lead you to a place of safety and bring you to a place of deep inner peace. You have to learn to trust that God's best is your best. Learn to tune into Him, learn to seek His presence, learn to express your desires to God. You also need to have an open heart to hear the desires of God's heart for you. Then you will be guided onto the path of righteousness.

Prayer Starter

Dear Lord, please help me to navigate the abyss of grief. Help me to find comfort in you and not in material things. Help me to focus on the positive and not the negative. Amen.

DAY 48

*Unless the Lord had given me help, I would soon have dwelt
in the silence of death.*

Psalm 94:17 (NIV)

I OFTEN REFLECT ON MY WILDERNESS PERIOD AND WONDER, how did I overcome that dark place? I call it the deep, dark pit. The truth is, without the grace of God I would have indeed dwelt in the silence of death. I would have stayed in darkness if my heart had not been open to His love for me, His comfort for me.

If it were not for the grace of God, I would probably be dead in a ditch somewhere. But I'm not – because I clung onto my faith, worshipped the Lord, prayed to the Lord and kept my spiritual life active by reading scripture daily. All these things were essential to my recovery and fundamental to choosing life over death.

However, people have also encouraged me to keep looking to the Cross and keep clinging onto the truths in the Bible. People have reminded me that life isn't just about grieving – there is more to life. People came and sat with me when I fell into a thousand pieces. Knowing that people were there beside me helped me to know that I was not alone. Knowing that people were praying for me helped me to move into the light and away from the all-consuming darkness.

The question I must ask you today is this, where do you put your struggles? Do you put them at the foot of the Cross? Or do you put them deep into your pocket? What does the Cross mean to you?

After my little one died it was a steep learning curve for me to learn to put my struggles on the Cross. Rather than stuffing them deep into my pocket, I pulled them out and pinned them to the Cross. I wore my pain on my sleeve and many people shied away from me and were scared. They did not want to be hit by such raw emotion. But if I had put my unresolved issues in my pocket, I would have started walking in a crippled manner. My body language would have revealed how tough life was. Instead, I radiated peace. I radiated God's love because God was freeing me from this pain, because He was comforting me and I allowed Him into my life so that I could be comforted.

I had to learn to surrender my unresolved issues, my pain, my sadness and my deep anguish at the foot of the Cross to be free. However, becoming free doesn't just happen overnight. It takes patience and perseverance. It takes up a lot of time.

Are you prepared to surrender your struggles to God? To lay them down at the Cross?

Prayer Starter

Dear Father God, help me to surrender my unresolved issues, my pain, my sadness and my deep anguish at the foot of the Cross. Help me to let go and let you in. Amen

DAY 49

Blessed are those who mourn, for they will be comforted.

Matthew 5:4 (NIV)

DENIAL IS THE STAGE AT WHICH OUR WORLD NO LONGER makes sense. We go into survival mode. We go into a state of shock and denial. It is God's way of allowing us to pace our grief. It allows us to feel grief, but only to the extent we can handle at the time. It allows God to come in and comfort us when we no longer know who to turn to. It helps us to cope with daily life after death occurs, enabling us to focus on the essentials.

For mothers who have lost babies before birth, denial enables them to focus on the task at hand, which is giving birth to their sleeping babies.

During the denial phase you start to ask yourself questions:

- Why me?
- What did I do wrong?
- Did something else go wrong?
- Did I deserve this?

This is you beginning to process grief in a healthy way as you set out on your soul-searching journey. Embrace it; don't run from it. It also gives the chance for God to answer your questions in the silence. It allows God to comfort you when you least expect it.

How do you think you managed to go through those early dark days? Do you think you did it in your own strength, or that God gave you the strength to crawl forward? Where did your comfort come from if it wasn't from the people around you?

God is the biggest comforter of all. He understands your pain and hates to see you suffer like that. He wants us to press into Him so that we can receive his comfort, His love. I know that Father God's comfort is far better than any comfort I have ever experienced in my life, simply because he knows what I need at that time and how to get me through the dark period. There were times when I know I wasn't walking but Father God was *carrying* me through the storm. He carried me because I couldn't walk, because the pain was too crippling to carry alone. That is when He is holding you and carrying you. When you can no longer move, God is there comforting you and helping you to move forward to that place of deep peace.

Prayer Starter

Dear Lord, please comfort me. Amen.

Prayer of My Heart

The Lord is with me
As I walk through the valley
Of death; I cry out to the Lord
And ask and pray
For my heart's desire to
Be shown,
As a small flicker of light
Beckons me to come –
A hope unseen
Between the flower buds.
O Lord, I cry,
Show me your light,
Show me your love,
Show me your comfort.
Show me your will, O Lord.
My God, my Saviour,
Guide me back
To the path of righteousness.
O Lord, my heart cries out.

DAY 50

In your anger do not sin, do not let the sun go down while
you are still angry, and do not give the devil a foothold.

Ephesians 4:26-27 (NIV)

BELIEVE IT OR NOT, BEING ANGRY BECAUSE OF YOUR SITU-
ation is a healthy stage to be in. It can be part of the healing process if
your anger is constructive. However, anger which remains can become a
very destructive force. If it isn't resolved it is a bridgehead for an invasion
by the enemy. Do not be afraid of your anger – although it may seem
unending, it will subside eventually. The more you truly feel anger, the
more it disintegrates and the more you will heal and become the person
God wants you to be. There are many emotions lurking beneath anger
that come out during this stage. Anger seems to have no limits. You start
questioning again:

- Why me?
- God, where are you in all of this?
- What is your purpose in all of this, God?
- God, why did you desert me?

Underneath all that anger is a simmering pot of endless, needless pain
that no-one wants to experience. But we live in a fallen world. When we
are angry we feel alone, abandoned and neglected as if we are battling
this storm on our own. You have to remember that in all of this, people
are afraid of grief. People are afraid of raw, unfiltered human anguish. It
scares them, therefore the natural response is to avoid it. So, you feel all
alone, like you are dealing with this pain on your own.

However, anger can be viewed as a strength. It can be an anchor in
the temporary, meaningless state called 'life after loss'. Grief can feel like
being adrift at sea, not connected to anyone or anything. You eventually
get angry at someone; maybe that person didn't attend the funeral, no
longer talks to you or is afraid to talk after your loved one has died.

Suddenly you have a structure – your anger towards them. This anger
becomes a bridge over the open sea, a connection from you to them. It is

something you cling onto. Perhaps it's a bridge connecting you to God – letting you cling onto Him as you work through the stages of grief.

Remember, anger is just another indication of the intensity of your love for that person or thing you have lost. In your anger do not sin, nor let that hope fade; let the light remain in you as you work through anger constructively.

Prayer Starter

Dear Lord, please help me to direct, then resolve, my anger in a constructive manner. Do not let me sin in my anger. Amen.

DAY 51

Do not be overcome by evil, but overcome evil with good.

Romans 12:21 (NIV)

WHEN THE MEDICAL STAFF TOLD ME THEY COULDN'T FIND my son's heartbeat, I begged God to let him live and let me die. I was asking Him to perform a miracle. Sometimes when a loved one is sick, you will bargain with God, begging him to spare this person's life and let them live. You might say, 'I will never be angry again,' or, 'I will do anything you want me to do, God, but please just let them live.'

After a loss, bargaining may take the form of a temporary truce. 'What if I devote the rest of my life to helping others? Then I can wake up from this nightmare and realise that this was all a terrible mistake. A bad dream.'

We get stuck in the endless treadmill of 'if only, if only, if only, what if, what if, what if…' It is only natural that we would want our life to be restored to normal, to what it was before we lost our loved one. We want to go back in time, to when we were in our comfort zone and didn't realise how fragile life can be. The problem with bargaining is that guilt is there, and guilt eats you alive. It is like a companion. It nags you: *if only I had done something differently…* It focuses on the invisible faults and what we think should have been done differently.

No-one wants to feel pain, so we bargain with it. We will do anything not to feel the pain of this loss. So, we may remain in the past trying to negotiate our way out of the hurt.

To remain in the past can be unhealthy, and there is also a risk of being stuck in grief. So be aware of the healthy ways of grieving. Don't let guilt trap you and make you feel worthless, like a failure. Allow yourself to bargain, but don't let it become an endless treadmill of what-ifs.

Bring your struggles to the Cross. Nail them to the Cross and let God in. Let God heal you. Let God comfort you. *Let go and let God in.*

Prayer Starter

*Dear Father God, teach me to be still. Help me to let go of my anger.
Help me to see that there is a purpose in this pain. Amen.*

DAY 52

I will turn their mourning into joy; I will comfort them and give them gladness for sorrow.

Jeremiah 31:13 (NIV)

REMEMBER THAT THE STAGES IN THE GRIEF CYCLE ARE often jumbled together. Grief is not a tidy process. It is messy. Sometimes after anger or bargaining or denial we enter the dreaded stage of depression. We are stuck in a dreadful reality from which we cannot escape.

Empty feelings present themselves, and grief enters our lives on a deeper level, deeper than we can imagine. People often think that depression is the incorrect response to losing someone, that depression is a mental illness, but it is important to understand that this is not the case. It is in fact an appropriate response to a great loss. People in this stage tend to withdraw from life, sitting in a thick fog of intense grief, wondering, perhaps, if there is any point in carrying on.

Depression is a normal and natural response to a great loss. It is more unusual *not* to go into a deep depression after someone dies. It is part of the process to restoration, to full healing, to complete wholeness. Yes, it can last a long time. Yes, you feel as if you are trapped in an endless cycle of despair, not knowing how long it will take to get out. But if you choose to move forward, step by step, eventually you will reach the end, and when you do that, it is so very refreshing. You look back at all those months that have gone by and you realise you have done it. You have coped. You have managed to get through one of the toughest times in your life. You are no longer walking wounded, a person fragmented, but now put back together into the new you. Some of your old ways stay with you, and new ways have also etched their way into your life. There is nothing wrong with that. You are going through the refiner's fire.

Prayer Starter

Dear Lord, please help me to go through the refiner's fire. Heal the brokenness inside me, comfort me when I weep. Turn my sorrow into gladness. Amen.

DAY 53

Brothers and sisters, we do not want you to be uninformed
about those who sleep in death, so that you do not grieve
like the rest of mankind, who have no hope.

1 Thessalonians 4:13 (NIV)

THIS IS THE STAGE WHERE YOU ACCEPT LOSS. IT IS ABOUT accepting the reality that life has carried on without your loved one. It is about recognising that your new reality has become permanent. It is a new norm with which we must learn to live. Acceptance is about finding peace in your new norm. It doesn't mean that everything is going to be alright all the time. You can still have bad days, but they are few and far between.

On the day after Sebby died, as I started to get on with my life and move on, I would feel guilty for laughing and smiling. But God does not want us to feel guilty. God does not want us to carry the burden of grief with us for the remainder of our lives. He wants us to move forward, carrying the lessons we learnt from our past experiences and integrating them with those learnt from new experiences. We can learn something from tragedy, move on and yet still carry forward the memories of our lost loved ones. Instead of denying our feelings as we did in the beginning, we should listen to our needs. We move, we change, we grow, we evolve.

At the end of the grieving journey, we may start to reach out to other people who have just experienced a loss. They are now the walking wounded, and we can now give them the courage and strength to face the murky waters of grief. We can give them hope because we have come through to the other side and so can they.

Once acceptance occurs, we may start to reach out to others and become involved in their lives once more. We start to invest in friendships again, when for a time we didn't do that because we were consumed by the all-powerful emotion of grief. We learn to live again. But give grief its time. It deserves it. You deserve to work through it. You deserve to be healed. You deserve to focus on yourself while you grapple with your new situation and learn to be at peace with your new norm.

Prayer Starter

Dear Lord, thank you for helping me to accept the loss. Thank you for healing my wounds, and for bringing the joy back into my life. Amen.

DAY 54

Be careful how you think,
your life is shaped by your thoughts.

Proverbs 4:23 (NIV)

'ATTITUDE' IS DEFINED AS A SETTLED WAY OF THINKING OR feeling about something or the environment around us. We each have attitudes. Some of these attitudes are developed in the environment that we live in. We can have a negative view of the world or a positive worldview. Even God's attitudes can influence our lives, especially when our own attitudes can lead us off the straight and narrow path.

What is our attitude in the face of adversity, grief, tragedy? How do we respond to grief? Do we respond to our troubles in a negative way? Do we curse God? Or do we praise God and trust the Lord that He will see us through this difficult patch? What do you do?

When we are faced with difficulties and end up in a wilderness, our natural response is to revert to the attitudes we grew up with. Coming from a non-Christian family, it would be easy to go back to those attitudes and abandon faith. The wilderness period is the stripping of all the layers to see what is really in our hearts. *Do we cry out to God in anger that he has taken away what was ours? Or do we put our trust in Him, and believe that His perfect plan is best?*

The only way for us to overcome the tragedy around us is by holding onto the good, godly attitudes. We win through by walking in the Spirit and by having a close relationship with God the Father. We do that through His word, praying and worshipping. The only way we can do this is by being open to God; by being receptive of His love, rather than pushing it away; by letting His word cleanse us from the inside out, letting it inhabit all the things that we do.

Life is about challenges; it is about difficulties. It is about facing them with zeal and joy, with a positive attitude rather than a negative one. I remember someone once telling me this and it stuck with me while I was grieving my lost son.

People will watch how you grieve, whether you are clinging onto God or turning your back on Him. What is it you want people to see? A strong faith or a faith that does not exist at all? So, with an attitude of being afraid of grief, I moved forward, albeit begrudgingly, trusting the Lord in the face of adversity and believing that He would see me through.

Prayer Starter

Dear Father God, help me to have a godly attitude. Teach me to overcome tragedy. Show me how to help your broken people. Take away this pain, Lord. Teach me so that I can be strong in you. Amen.

DAY 55

The Word of God is alive and active, sharper than a double-edged sword.

Hebrews 4:12 (NIV)

BEFORE SEBASTIAN DIED, I READ THE BIBLE PERHAPS TWO OR three times per week. Afterwards, I started reading the Bible daily, particularly when I started the second year of my grief journey. I also started doing Bible studies to deal with the negative emotions inside of me. I made it a priority in my life and noticed a difference – if I didn't read the Bible or have my daily quiet time with God, then the day would go pear-shaped. If I did read the Bible and spend a large chunk of time walking to work in prayer, I found the day would go better and I wouldn't have this fear haunting me. It was quite simple: I knew Jesus was with me and I opened my heart for him to lead me through the day.

I downloaded the *NIV 365-Day Devotional Reading Plan*. To be honest, in the beginning I found it a burden to read daily. But as the days progressed and turned into a month, I found myself seeking to read the Bible more and more, and going beyond the plan. I was hungry for God's word and noticed a significant spiritual growth. With this growth came healing. God was speaking to my broken heart and slowly binding up my wounds. What a miracle!

The One Year Bible is also an excellent tool, as it solves the problem of what to read each day. For every day of the year there are four readings: Old Testament, New Testament, Psalms and Proverbs. With this Bible, you can start any day of the year, and if you have limited time you can choose to read either the Old Testament, New Testament, Psalms or Proverbs reading, or choose two. This is brilliant, inspirational, practical, helpful, spiritual and achievable.

In a notebook, I would like to challenge you to write one Bible verse that speaks to you every day. I mean *every* day. You will notice that God will speak to you every day if you ask Him. The key to hearing God's voice is being open to hear His spoken word. Do you want to hear God's voice? Then let Him speak to your heart. Don't avoid it.

I cannot stress enough how this simple action of doing Bible studies, writing key Bible verses down and developing a personal relationship with Father God saved my life – and it can save yours too. It grows your faith and is a blessing beyond measure. The Father of the universe can speak to a broken wretch like me every day and encourage me and build me up *every single day of my life.* How amazing!

Prayer Starter

Dear Father God, help me to place you as priority in my life. Help me to look up to you and not at myself. Amen.

DAY 56

For to us a child is born, to us a son is given, and the government will be on his shoulders. And he will be called Wonderful Counsellor.

Isaiah 9:6 (NIV)

PEOPLE OFTEN THINK THAT COUNSELLING IS FOR WEAK people – people with problems. But let's face it... who doesn't have problems? God has created many kinds of people: writers, musicians, teachers, counsellors. The list goes on. If we have a toothache we go to the dentist.

So, if we have an ongoing issue, or have experienced a traumatic event, Father God has given us the option to seek counselling. The counsellor is neutral, someone who lets us talk. While we are talking in a safe environment, we can learn about our negative views of the world and in a healthy manner purge ourselves of all the negativity that is in us. Yes, counselling is tough, but it is there for us – so use it. Don't be afraid of it. Going to a counsellor to help us sift through the complex cycle of life's issues is not something we have to be ashamed of.

There are many different types of counsellors. There are Christian counsellors, non-Christian counsellors, specialist counsellors. Above all we must remember one thing: the Holy Spirit is the greatest counsellor we have. The Holy Spirit can counsel our hearts and help us get to the root of the issue with a depth and clarity like no other counsellor.

If you do decide to go down the path of counselling, then I recommend that it goes alongside sitting at the foot of the Cross. True healing can only occur at the foot of the Cross. There you can *surrender* all your struggles to the Lord. It is where the Lord meets you and heals you. I call the foot of the Cross the *Lord's Counselling Chamber*. This is where you purge yourself of all that negativity that is inside of you and you release it to Him. Admittedly, it is not a quick fix. It can take days, weeks, months or years to be completely healed and to feel completely free. I am still a work in progress.

I decided to go for counselling because I was afraid to be stuck in grief for the rest of my life. I didn't want to go on medication. I knew that would not work because I knew where my issues came from. A pill can't fix the humdrum of issues in your life; it can only numb the pain. It cannot heal the root issues of the heart. Only God the Father can heal us if we are open to receiving healing. Surrender to God's plan and accept that He knows best.

Prayer Starter

Dear Father God, let your Holy Spirit who lives in me speak to me and heal me from the wounds of my despair. Amen.

DAY 57

But the wisdom that comes from heaven is first of all pure,
then peace-loving, considerate, submissive, full of mercy and
good fruit, impartial and sincere.

James 3:17 (NIV)

COUNSELLING HELPED ME BECAUSE:

- I was desperate;
- I found the right counsellor at the right time; and
- the counselling went together with the renewal of my spiritual walk. I was learning to pray again, learning to read the word, learning to study the word, learning to spend time in God's presence, learning to humble myself and surrender to His will again and again and again.

Counselling without spiritual renewal is like a kitchen without a rubbish bag. Counselling can identify your issues, their origin and your dysfunctional responses to them. The problem is, if you don't have somewhere like the sanctuary to take your negative emotions then you may end up problem-centred and worse off than when you started.

So, you may be attracted to counselling to help you with your issues. I hope that you are – but I also hope that you are realistic about the exercise. It's all a bit tougher and costlier than you think and takes a lot longer than a short walk to the corner shop.

The Holy Spirit is the best counsellor.

Let me just reiterate that: the Holy Spirit helps us best in our deepest need, in our time of trial when our hearts are open to receive his guidance. He is the Comforter (Counsellor, Helper, Intercessor, Advocate and Standby).

The Helper, the Holy Spirit, whom the Father will send in
my name, he will teach you all things and bring to your
remembrance all that I have said to you.

John 14:26 (ESV)

The moment we get tired in the waiting, God's Spirit is right alongside helping us along. If we don't know how or what to pray, it doesn't matter. He knows. He does our praying in and for us, making prayer out of our wordless sighs, our aching groans. He knows us far better than we know ourselves; He knows our present condition and keeps us before God. That's why we can be so sure that every detail in our lives of love for God is worked into something good.[7]

And that's why we need the Holy Spirit so much. He is the essential working component in this whole exercise, counselling or no counselling.

Prayer Starter

Dear Father God, heal me, please. I need you. Amen.

---

[7] See Romans 8:26-28

DAY 58

The fruit of the Spirit is ... self-control.
Galatians 5:22-23 (NIV)

DIET. DIET. DIET. FOOD. FOOD. FOOD. WHY AM I TALKING about diet? Diet is also a key component for our physical, emotional and spiritual wellbeing. What we feed on and take in is what we become. What we put in our mouth can affect us emotionally, physically and spiritually. God wants us to honour our bodies, and that includes what we put in our mouths.

When I lost my son, for a long time I couldn't eat anything. I couldn't put anything into my mouth. I wanted to starve. I wanted to die. Why? Because I felt like life wasn't worth living. But as the days turned into weeks, and weeks into months, I began to eat again. However, this time round it became an unhealthy eating habit. I would stuff my mouth endlessly with junk food, or just any food I could lay my hands on, so I could fill the empty void inside me. I ate to fill the loneliness inside me and to close the wound within. But does this method of overeating work? Does it resolve anything? *It didn't.*

When I was overeating, I started gaining weight, which fuelled the negative spiral I was entering. It deepened my depression. I felt like the biggest failure. I could see huge, yucky flabs of flesh around and I felt deeply discouraged. I saw a failed life and felt like a failure, someone who couldn't get a grip on life. The poor eating habit made me feel worse about myself. It lowered my self-esteem and it fuelled my self-hatred.

In contrast, when I started eating healthily, lost weight and exercised, the negative spiral of my life gradually began to lift. It enabled me to look at myself properly. We are very much what we eat. Poor diet leads to depression, but a healthy, well-balanced diet helps us on the way to wholeness.

In the same way, poor spiritual diet can cause our souls to be sick. If we don't feed ourselves daily with God's word, we neglect a spiritual food vital to our health as spiritually needy people. We become mere natural beings, not relying on God, running from one crisis to the next. And then wondering, 'Where are you, God, in all of this?'

The key lesson here is to eat a well-balanced and healthy diet. We need to avoid poor foods that are rich in sugar. We also read God's word daily, which is food for us spiritually. God will provide for our needs. He does not want us to suffer. He wants us to have peace.

Prayer Starter

Dear Father God, help me to rely on you. Help me to treat my body with the respect it deserves. Teach me to not allow myself to sink into the pit of despair. Help me to sing praises to you. Amen.

DAY 59

Bodily exercise profits a little, but godliness is profitable for all things, having promise of the life that now is and of that which is to come.

1 Timothy 4:8 (NIV)

WHY BOTHER TO EXERCISE? WHAT IS THE USE OF IT? MY body doesn't want to exercise. My body just wants to lie down in a tiny hole and forget that I exist. I don't have the energy to do anything. That is how I felt after my son died. I couldn't be bothered to exercise anymore because I didn't see the point. But a lack of exercise led to a decline in how I felt about and viewed myself. I saw myself as a failure because I couldn't do anything. I couldn't be bothered.

I struggled to maintain a good daily routine of talking to God, because I couldn't find peace within myself. I couldn't rest at home because I was lying around all the time, moping. I struggled to see any point in life. Then one day I saw the flabs of rolling flesh on my body, and that made me determined to do something different.

I planned to walk to work, and to start running several times a week to establish a good daily routine. You see, when you exercise, you release 'happy hormones'. I realised this after running for several weeks in a row. I noticed how my mood lifted. This, together with a well-balanced diet, enabled me to come out of that negative spiral of defeat, despair and failure, and work my way back up the ladder to see that I was not, and I am not, a failure. I am Father God's daughter.

When I started to walk to work each day, I used that time to speak to God and this became an important part of my daily routine. I noticed that if I didn't walk and spend time with God, my day would go pear-shaped. If I did walk and run three times per week, I felt like I was on top of the world. I felt as if I could overcome any struggle with God's help.

Physical exercise releases a natural antidepressant endorphin into the blood system. Physical exercise can help us to overcome anxiety, panic attacks, despair and feeling useless because our body does not function.

While I am living, I will honour my temporary body by exercising, as this promotes physical, emotional and spiritual wellbeing. The negative downward spiral becomes a positive upward spiral, and you can walk and pray. The spiritual dimension can be combined with the physical and then you have the best of both worlds. You see God's creation and it gives you hope, a longing to want to spend more time in His presence. It boosts your energy levels.

Prayer Starter

Dear Father God, help me to have the boldness to exercise. Help me to be diligent in looking after myself in all areas so that I can be free. Amen.

God Weeps

Silent tears roll,
Every tear counts;
God weeps with me.
I feel like a rabbit caught in a
Car's headlight, frozen to the spot,
Not knowing how to move forward.
Look to the Cross,
Sit in God's presence.
Silent tears roll,
Every tear counts;
God weeps with me.

DAY 60

I turned to the Master God, asking for an answer – praying earnestly, fasting from meals, wearing rough penitential burlap, and kneeling in the ashes. I poured out my heart, baring my soul to God.

Daniel 9:3 (NIV)

FASTING IS AN IMPORTANT ELEMENT TO OUR SPIRITUAL walk. Why do we need to fast? So that we can break the spiritual strongholds in our life that we can't just break by praying or by speaking to a Christian counsellor. Fasting can enable us to have a closer, more dependable relationship with our Heavenly Father.

I know that fasting is hard. To do it, I would suggest easing into it slowly. Don't do a three- to five-day fast if you've never fasted before. Make an easy achievable goal. If you set up a difficult goal, you will be setting yourself up for failure. Then you won't see the point in fasting.

After my son died, I was not able to fast, because I wasn't spiritually well enough. I was emotionally fragile and I was totally broken. Eventually, after I started to heal and feel emotionally whole, I could start fasting to address besetting sins within me. I could fast once a week. Although it was a challenge, I observed how I drew closer to God's will for my life, how I overcame various persistent sins in my life that had dogged me for years. Fasting also cleared my mind and helped me think with greater clarity. I felt energised and spiritually renewed. It was a great encouragement to me. And I was experiencing emotional and spiritual healing on a whole new level.

I see fasting as an essential spiritual discipline, but it was also a major part of my detox program, allowing my body to dump the build-up of toxins that we all face in this modern, cancer-inducing age of polluted air, water and food.

There are nine reasons to fast:

- obedience to God's word;
- humility;
- overcoming temptations;

- purification from sin;
- recognition of our weaknesses before God;
- God's support to accomplish His will in times of crisis;
- for guidance;
- for clearer understanding and divine revelation; and
- for exercising authority over the enemy.

Number one fasting tip: if you feel hungry, drink something such as water – *not alcohol.*

Prayer Starter

Dear Father God, please purify me. Please help me to be still in your presence. Help me to focus on you. Amen.

DAY 61

*But solid food is for the mature, who by constant use have
trained themselves to distinguish good from evil.*

Hebrews 5:14 (NIV)

WE ARE ALL CREATURES OF HABIT; WE ARE MADE THAT WAY
by God. Habit is second nature. It is the law deep within us. One of the
secrets to success is to establish and maintain good (godly) daily habits,
and to starve bad (ungodly) habits. A habit should be consistent. It is
about being consistent in all areas of your life.

Happiness isn't built on bad and ungodly foundations. It is built on
good and godly foundations. It is built on consistency. It is being aware
of what is right and what is wrong. Here is my story of how a change in
my habits changed the course of my life.

When I was married to my ex-husband, I drifted away from God. I
actively stopped seeking God. My daily habits became a distant memory.
I stopped reading God's word each day. I stopped praying and I stopped
exercising. I stopped believing that Father God cared about me and my
situation. My ex-husband became abusive, and steadily stripped away
my self-worth and confidence. In my crisis, I no longer knew what I had
to do. I was so far away from Father God, I felt that I didn't deserve his
love anymore. I felt as if I couldn't go to him for help anymore. I remained
far away from Him until one day I heard Him speak to me: 'Come to me
all you who are weary and burdened, and I shall give you rest.'[8] Once I
heard that voice, I knew I had to go and that God would be by my side,
that I was not alone.

I moved into a woman's shelter where I began to establish good and
godly daily habits. I would go for daily walks which helped me to pray
to Father God and to hear from Him. I would read God's word and I
would worship Him every day. God was with me there during that crisis
and led me back onto the path of righteousness. In fact, I am never alone.
The Holy Trinity of God the Father, God the Son and God the Holy Spirit
is with me. So, when I fall, I have three persons in one mighty Lord lift

---

[8] Matthew 11:28 (NIV)

me up and carry me. When I am weary, He fills me with His love and strength so that I can keep going.

The fact that I realised that God was with me all the time helped me when my son Sebastian died. Because I had already established a good routine of godly habits of reading the Bible, worshipping the Lord and praying to Him, I was able to put it into practice when I had so much turmoil inside me.

It is hard to see the joy in a negative, bad situation. Yet when you put your focus on Father God rather than your own situation, you begin to heal. You begin to humble yourself before Him.

Habit is especially useful if we want to be in a close relationship with Father God. It helps us to be established firmly into our roots and beliefs. It helps us to spiritually focus on what He wants us to do.

Father God wants His children to be happy, consistent people who have a well-balanced godly life. He does not want us to live in chaos. He does not want us to suffer. Having good daily habits will help us in the long term. This helps us to focus on the more important things in life and helps us to prioritise things. It creates a safe environment for us, which is what our bodies crave.

Prayer Starter

Dear Father God, teach me to be still in every situation. Fill me with your joy. Amen.

DAY 62

Therefore if you have any encouragement from being united with Christ, if any comfort from his love, if any common sharing in the Spirit, if any tenderness and compassion, then make my joy complete by being like-minded, having the same love, being one in spirit and of one mind. Do nothing out of selfish ambition or vain conceit. Rather, in humility value others above yourselves, not looking to your own interests but each of you to the interests of the others.

Philippians 2:1-4 (NIV)

OFTEN WHEN PEOPLE ARE IN THE WILDERNESS, THEY withdraw from life. They don't think they'll ever come out of it. I didn't think I'd overcome it. During my wilderness time, I spent most of my time in complete solitude, largely withdrawn, struggling to go out with people. I wrote to purge myself of all the negative emotions crashing around in my body. It was therapy for me. How I was feeling wasn't for the whole world to read about. I never had any intention of sharing my grief with anyone. I didn't think anyone would want to read about grief, despair, loss, depression, panic attacks, anxiety and a whole host of other issues. Who would want to read that? What on earth do I have that can help others to overcome their issues?

I have courage and the Holy Trinity within me. I am not alone, and I want to radiate Father God's love. Father God, who helped me to overcome my wounded spirit, will enable me to help others through their pain. Father God, who showed me that I am loved regardless of my faults, wants to communicate His conquering love through my words.

When I shared my 'Sebby' manuscript with a friend, it had such an impact on them, that they encouraged me and helped me with all the stages to get my book published. They saw a ministry growing within me. They saw that I could help other people. The reality was that I just wanted to hide in my woman's cave, but my friends enabled me to release a dream that I didn't think was possible.

The final stage of healing is when the Lord enables us to help others. The best person to help someone who has lost a child to stillbirth is another person who has experienced stillbirth. If we are in a wilderness period ourselves after the loss of a child, or any other kind of grief, then the testimony of someone who has come through that experience thirty months later is of great encouragement to us. This is because it shows that even in our darkest moments there is hope and we can overcome any adversity that is thrown at us. If it is too painful to walk, then we must crawl. If we can't walk at all, then we should simply let God carry us.

Prayer Starter

Dear Father God, heal me so that I can help others. Use me as your vessel for the broken-hearted. Teach me your ways, Father God. Hold me, Father. Carry me, Father, for I am weak. Amen.

DAY 63

And with that Jesus breathed on them and said: receive the
Holy Spirit.

John 20:22 (NIV)

THE HOLY SPIRIT IS A PERSON, THE THIRD PERSON OF THE
Trinity, not just some mystical force. There are many different views of
who the Holy Spirit is, but the Bible teaches us through many scriptures
that the Holy Spirit is God, for example, in Acts 5:3-4. We also know
that the Holy Spirit is God because He possesses the same characteristics
as God. For example, His omnipresence is seen in Psalm 139:

> *Where can I go from your Spirit? Where can I flee from your*
> *presence? If I go up to the heavens you are there; if I make*
> *my bed in the depths, you are there.*

Psalm 139:7-8

Then in 1 Corinthians we see the characteristic of omniscience in the
Holy Spirit:

> *But God has revealed it to us by His Spirit. The Spirit*
> *searches all things, even the deep things of God. For who*
> *among men knows the thoughts of man except the man's*
> *spirit within him? In the same way no one knows the*
> *thoughts of God except the Spirit of God.*

1 Corinthians 2:10-11

Finally, the Bible tells us that the Holy Spirit is a divine person – a
being with a mind, emotions and will. He thinks and knows,[9] He can be
grieved,[10] He intercedes for us[11] and He makes decisions according to His
will.[12]

---

[9] See 1 Corinthians 2:10
[10] See Ephesians 4:30
[11] See Romans 8:26-27
[12] See 1 Corinthians 12:7-11

The Holy Spirit is therefore God, the third person of the Trinity. As God, the Holy Spirit can truly function as the comforter and counsellor that Jesus promised he would be.[13]

The Holy Spirit is everywhere. He can intercede for us when we make bad decisions, or when we are at death's door; He can help us to face our issues. The Holy Spirit is our comforter and counsellor. We just have to be open to His word and not be afraid of it.

For someone who is in a crisis, you simply need more of the Holy Spirit. For someone who is grieving, you just need more of the Holy Spirit. For someone who is suffering from depression, you need to call upon the Holy Spirit to fill your being. Whatever the issues, adversity or tragedy you are facing, you need more of Him. You need Him for guidance, but not just for guidance – you also depend on Him as your number one counsellor and comforter. Don't be afraid of the Holy Spirit. Seek Him and your reward will be great.

When he, the Spirit of truth comes, he will guide you into all the truth.

John 16:13

Prayer Starter

Dear Father God, teach me your ways. Guide me in your paths of righteousness. Amen.

---

[13] See John 14:16-26

DAY 64

You will show me the path of life. In Your presence is
fullness of joy. At your right hand are pleasures forevermore.

Psalm 16:11 (NIV)

IT IS IMPORTANT TO SPEND TIME IN THE PRESENCE OF
Father God. Without Him, where would we be? God is our refuge, our
ever-present help in trouble. The problem with our society today is
technology – the humbug of technology used everywhere. *Distraction!*
And what is the distraction? It is an unhealthy obsession with technology
and its abuse. You probably understand my gist. We have so many
distractions that we no longer find the time – or are not *willing* to find
the time – to spend with the Lord. Everything else seems to be more
important.

I learnt quickly that Father God is important, especially when I
plummeted into my wilderness hole. I knew that there was no way up or
out except for trusting that His unfailing love would see me through.
Why? Because nothing else seemed to help. Nothing else seemed to work.
There was no quick fix to what I was facing. When I was pregnant with
my son, the only option I had was to trust that God would provide for
my every need and that He would look after my son's need. I was
powerless to find a quick-fix solution, which we so often want to have in
a world where everything seems to be at our fingertips.

So while I lived in the shelter, I developed a daily and godly habit of
reading my Bible, spending time in the presence of Father God and
praying to Him. My prayer time would often be the first thing in the
morning, and then throughout the day as the Holy Spirit led me. I also
prayed often for the Holy Spirit to guide me throughout the day and to
help me face whatever lay before me. I trusted that He would guide me,
and lived by faith, believing that Father God would provide for me. It
was a childlike faith, pure and innocent, yet strong, and the only way
forward for my life.

I want to encourage you to develop a good habit of spending an hour
a day in the presence of Father God. As you set a regular time aside each
day to spend with Him, you will see how he will grow you spiritually,

and help you to overcome any issue that you face that day. What you feed grows. What you don't feed starves.

Prayer Starter

Dear Lord, please take away any distraction in my life so that I may put my focus on you and seek your presence all the time.

DAY 65

*Then Hannah prayed and said: 'My heart rejoices in the
Lord, in the Lord my horn is lifted high. My mouth boasts
over my enemies, for I delight in your deliverance.'*

1 Samuel 2:1 (NIV)

PRAYER IS A SIMPLE EXPRESSION OF GRATITUDE TO GOD IN worship, but it can also be a plea for help. It is the biggest communication channel between God and yourself. Use it! Often people are frightened to pray. Why? Because they think they don't know how to pray like the person next to them who seems to pray with so much emotion. But prayer is simply allowing yourself to be vulnerable to God and thanking him with a humble heart. It is about unveiling yourself before Him, and believing that He truly loves you and that He has a perfect plan for your life.

When I was pregnant with Sebastian, I would pray to God every day. This became a good, godly habit. It enabled me to deepen my relationship with Him. It allowed me to be open to His word and to hear that soft *rhema* voice of the Lord. The daily habit of praying established a good routine for me when tragedy did strike. But was it enough?

Prayer is essential. Prayer helps us to overcome obstacles that we might not otherwise be able to overcome. Prayer is about being open to God our Father. Prayer is about surrendering your struggles at the foot of the Cross and allowing Father God's soft voice to enter your dwelling place. It is about being silent before Him, but also willing to hear what He has to say to you. For that you need to have an open heart to receive His word and His love.

Prayer allows you to be vulnerable when you are truly open and honest about your emotions. It is about humbling yourself before God, and believing that He can provide for your needs, while it is also an expression of thanksgiving.

We live in troubling times – we all need to learn how to pray. We need to pray more frequently, more openly, and not be afraid of *learning* how to pray. God delights in His children who pray. There is no correct way, nor is there a wrong way. If you are earnestly seeking God through prayer, you can't have got it wrong.

God hears your prayers and will not forsake you. He loves you and wants to be in a deeper relationship with you. As for me, I want to have a deeper and more fulfilling relationship with my Father God.

Prayer Starter

Dear Father God, speak to me. Let me hear your voice. In you I put my trust. Amen.

DAY 66

Be still, and know that I am God, I will be exalted among the nations, I will be exalted in the earth. The Lord of hosts is with us. The God of Jacob is our refuge. Selah.

Psalm 46:10-11 (NIV)

WHAT IS A SANCTUARY? IT IS A SAFE PLACE WHERE WE CAN unload our burdens and unveil ourselves at the foot of the Cross. It is a place where we can meet with God. It does not necessarily have to be in a church building. It can be anywhere that is safe for you. It can be in your room; it can be in a church; it can be sitting by a river; it can be sitting in your favourite armchair. The list of possibilities is endless.

Why is finding daily sanctuary with God so important? If we don't make it a priority, our faith will decline and we will eventually fall away from faith. If we don't have daily sanctuary time with Him, our spiritual walk could eventually die. This scares me the most because without faith and hope, without a spiritual walk, without spending time with Father God daily, we become easy prey for deception.

The thing I realised after my son died was that I don't just want to rely on Father God only in the emergency; I want to rely on Him all the time. I want to be dependent on Him consistently. I want to be His daughter. I don't want to go from crisis to crisis wondering why I am always in a crisis. It therefore becomes a priority for me to rely on Father God all the time, not only so that I could develop that open communication channel with Him, but also to nail my struggles on the Cross, that I could be free. Freedom for me meant not to be always burdened with deep grief.

God does not want His children to be burdened with deep grief. He wants us to be free, so that we can help others in similar situations, so that we can be at peace, so that we can be an example to others of His love for us.

The sanctuary is also a place where you can just quietly read God's word, worship Him, hear His voice and pray. Our Father God loves it when we seek refuge in Him and seek His presence. He delights in this and rewards us for spending time with Him. He loves us and wants to show that to us. Be open to hearing Father God's voice, to spending time with Him every day. It is important for your spiritual walk, as well as for the deepening of your faith.

Prayer Starter

Dear Lord, please help me to find refuge in you. Help me to seek your presence so that I may feel your love seep through my wall. Amen.

DAY 67

I thank you, God, from a full heart,
I'm writing the book on your wonders.
I'm whistling, laughing, and jumping for joy,
I'm singing your song, High God.

Psalm 9:1-2 (MSG)

EVERYONE CAN WRITE. ANYONE CAN DO IT IF THEY PUT their pen to paper and just let the unconscious part of their mind take them into a world they never could have imagined. Writing was my most valuable therapy. It was a form of purging. I would gather the emotions of grief within me and they would consume me so much that I felt as if I was suffocating. I knew from experience that the only way to get rid of them was to write them down. So, write I did!

Writing became part of my daily life. I would write and I would cry. I would purge myself from the intense emotions of grief. It helped me. I have written so much in the last years, it is hard to imagine what life would be like without writing.

The point I am trying to make is, don't be afraid to try and write down what you are feeling. Maybe it will help you, maybe it won't. Maybe if you write, you can scrunch the paper into a ball and throw it away. Often, I would write and then delete, or save and not share it with anyone.

Write *something,* paint *something,* do *something* with your grief – but don't bottle it up. Don't let it fester into a big, ugly wound. Let it go. Give it all to Father God. Surrender it to Him. Set it all down at the foot of the Cross and He will heal you. You will be free. You will become whole with time. It won't happen overnight. It is a long, drawn-out process, but worth it.

Sometimes I would write down prayer letters as a form of communication with God when nothing else worked – when I was afraid to use my voice because I was so angry; angry at him for taking away everything that was dear to me. But Father God's love and compassion began seeping into my world and I began to heal.

Prayer Starter

Dear Father God, please teach me how to pray. Teach me to let go. Teach me to trust you. Teach me your ways. Help me to be free. Use me as your vessel, for I am yours and I am not afraid. Amen.

DAY 68

God is spirit, and his worshippers must worship in Spirit and in truth.

John 4:24 (NIV)

WORSHIP TOWARDS GOD IS BORN IN OUR HEARTS. IT THEN rolls over to our bodies. Worship is about surrendering of hands to God. It is about the bowing of the head towards the Son. Worship is about letting go and being completely free in God's presence. It's about having our shame, guilt, despair and frustrations stripped away before Him, and making Him the number one priority in our lives. It is about praising God in all circumstances, whether they are good or bad.

I have found that people confuse worship with singing. Worship is more than just singing. It can be part of our daily devotional time and it has many different forms. It can be about exalting the Lord, or it can be the lifting of hands. It can be about speaking out firm confessions and statements such as, 'Father God, I worship you for who you are. I thank you for your great love for me, and I thank you for your word to me today.'

I usually open my hands or lift my hands up in an act of surrendering to Father God's will, saying, 'Father, I am all yours; your will be done in my life.' It is amazing how this simple physical act of surrendering to Him can lift us up out of our stifling pride, transforming us to be humble before Him and before others. He can lift us out of despair or out of our smug pride when we humble ourselves before Him. This is so very refreshing.

When Father God sees our heart of worship, He can draw us near to Him. We can often feel the Holy Spirit speak to our hearts when we surrender ourselves completely to His will. It is revitalising. It brings hope to a dying heart. It brings hope to a person filled with utter despair. It brings hope in the darkness. It allows us to see that God is far bigger and greater than our problems.

Prayer Starter

Dear Father, help me to surrender myself as I worship you freely. Speak to me as I worship you. Amen

DAY 69

*Worship the Lord with gladness; come before him with
joyful songs.*

Psalm 100:2 (NIV)

GOD IS LOOKING FOR A HEART OF WORSHIP EVEN WHEN
things go terribly wrong. When my son died in 2014, was I going to curse
God for taking him away? Or was I going to praise Him? How would
you react to a situation that is totally out of your control? Will you lift
your hands in surrender to God in worship, and say, 'Father, you are in
control of my life and of my circumstances. You are far bigger than the
issues I am facing. I worship you even in the face of darkness.'?

I didn't know how I was going to react, but I decided that my best
option was to worship God despite my circumstances. The reason was, I
knew that He was bigger than the problems in my life. I knew that He
could lift me out of the pit of despair, if I surrendered to His will, if I
surrendered my son to God daily. It was the process of humbling myself
before the Lord, and praising Him, and thanking Him even in my
darkness.

People are watching how you react in the face of deep tragedy. They
observe you. They watch you like a hawk! In my case, my younger sister
was observing me to see how I would react to my situation of losing my
son. Every day, I would sing worship songs to God, exalting Him and
thanking Him for my circumstances.[14]

My sister asked me one day, 'Why are you singing to Father God and
thanking Him for taking away your son?'

My response was simple, though filled with a deep, painful trembling:
'Sebastian is safe in the arms of Jesus. He doesn't have to experience
suffering like you and me. He's in the best place he can be. So, I am
thanking God because my son is safe.'

Now, each time I am sad, my younger sister puts her arms around me
and reminds me of this truth: *Sebastian is safe with Jesus.* I am a witness

---

[14] See 1 Thessalonians 5:18

to her and to other people, no matter what the circumstances are in my life.

I want to be a *faithful* witness, radiating our Father's love to the world and experiencing the peace that He can give me through my circumstances. God is faithful, and His love fills all the dark corners in my heart and heals me. God can heal you too; just be open to receiving it.

Prayer Starter

Dear Father God, I lift up all honour and all glory to you. To you I worship. I thank you for every situation I am in. Thank you, Lord. You are a great God. Amen.

Tsunami of Love

Father is love, has always been love from the very beginning.
Though I did not know, Father loved me;
Yes, he loves me still and forevermore.
Every pore in my body screamed, I do not deserve this love;
I am afraid to be loved, my walls are high.
No-one can break them, or can they?
Why does the love I experienced hurt so much?

Slowly, with time and persistence
The walls started crumbling around me and
The soldiers of protection in me
Started shutting their eyes
To my wounded spirit,
Commenced with hammers
To break down this sturdy wall of hurt
That was built around my wounded heart.

Through this crack in the wall
The voice of my Father came
As sweet as the sound of angels singing,
Calling out my name, Hannah, I am here
And I love you just the same.
Don't be afraid, my child, let your guard down.
Come to me, my child, lie in the comfort of my arms.
You will be comforted, my rivers of love
Will flow through your vessels
So that you can be complete by my love.

The innocence of Father's love
Healed my weary soul,
Showing me to a place of sweet rest.
His love, so secure and so pure,
Is where I want to be –
Radiating it for the world to see.
Father is in me, and he loves me
Just the way I am.
With all my faults, I am his

And he dwells within me.
He wants me.

Father calls my name:
Hannah, sweet child, let go.
Let me in, don't be afraid
Of love vaster than the blue oceans,
Deeper than the trenches of endless hurt.
Let love flow.
I learn to accept myself.
I am free.
I am my Father's daughter.

DAY 70

Go to the Lord for help, and worship him continually.

1 Chronicles 16:11 (NIV)

WHY WOULD I WORSHIP WHEN THINGS ARE SO GLUM? WHEN there is so much turmoil in my life? Father God said to me once, 'Run to me. Grace will carry you home.'

I know for a fact that with all my turmoil – with all my angst, anger, despair and grief – I will not find peace unless I rely on God for strength. Unless I surrender to Him and humble myself before my Father God, I won't experience it. Therefore, I worship the Lord, so that I can have peace inside my heart.

People observe how you react in the time of trial. My sisters observed me and one of them once told me, 'I want to have what you have: peace.' How do you get to the that point of peace? Simply by accepting the Lord's will in your life, exalting Him and believing wholeheartedly that God is in control despite the circumstances.

I knew from the onset after losing Sebastian that I did not want to be stuck in grief – quite frankly, because this intense grief scared me. It filled me with a fear that I would be trapped in it forever. I made a conscious decision to praise the Lord, so that I could get out of the dark murky waters of grief quickly. I knew that peace would only come if I surrendered my struggles to the Cross. The process is about humbling yourself before the Cross and knowing within your heart that Father God can pull you through the chaos of your life, from darkness into light.

It was hard in the beginning to praise the Lord. I didn't do it because I wanted to. I did it with a sole purpose: that I would not be stuck in grief. I did it begrudgingly. I did it to crawl forward. I ran to God because I had nowhere to turn and because I knew that only He could comfort me. No-one else could comfort me. He helped me up. His grace carried me home.

Prayer Starter

Dear Father God, help me to respond to my grief journey in a positive way. Help me to lean on you for understanding. Help me to focus on you. Amen.

DAY 71

*But since we belong to the day, let us be sober, putting on
faith and love as a breastplate, and the hope of salvation as a
helmet.*

1 Thessalonians 5:8 (NIV)

TO OVERCOME DIFFICULT SITUATIONS IN OUR LIVES, AND TO
conquer the lies of the enemy, we receive spiritual weapons from God to
support us on our spiritual walk. When we choose to use them, the
benefits are huge.

I heard a story once. It was about a little girl who was with her
granddad. Granddad said, 'There are two types of wolves. One is evil.'
He pictured anger, envy, sorrow, regret, greed, arrogance, self-pity, guilt,
resentment, inferiority, lies, false pride, superiority and ego. 'The other
wolf is good.' He pictured joy, love, hope, serenity, humility, kindness,
benevolence, empathy, generosity, truth, compassion and faith. 'These
two wolves had a fight.' The little girl asked Granddad who won the
fight. The granddad was silent for some time, then answered, *'Whoever
you feed wins the fight.'*

You see, you have the same fight inside of you. If you feed the wolf
with all the negative emotions, then that wolf will win; but if you feed
the good wolf with all the positive emotions, then this wolf will win.
Which wolf do you want to win in your life? Are you hungry to live a life
of peace, filled with compassion and love?

There are four main spiritual weapons that can be used against the
lies of the enemy.

- *God's word.* When we read scripture every day, we are nourishing
  ourselves with spiritual food. It helps us to focus on God, and it
  gives us practical examples of how to overcome situations that
  happen in day-to-day life.
- *Praise.* We thank God for the situation that we are in, which lifts
  us out of a negative spiral, as our focus is on Father God rather
  than ourselves.

- *Worship.* We exalt the Lord and lift our hands in surrender to His will; it is the act of humbling ourselves in His presence.
- *Prayer.* This is the open communication channel between you and God. It is where we can praise Him, worship Him and present our requests to Him. It is also a time when we can be silent before Him and hear His soft voice (*rhema* word) speak to us, amid the chaos of day-to-day life.

When we read our Father God's word daily, praise Him daily, worship Him daily and pray to Him daily, we develop a deeper and more personal relationship with Him. It helps us to shift our focus from ourselves onto Him. It helps us to embrace the negative situations in our lives with a godly attitude.

Stay plugged into God's love. Stay on the wave of love. There is hope.

Prayer Starter

Dear Father God, help me to stay plugged into you. For my hope is in you. Amen.

DAY 72

*Ask and it will be given to you; seek and you will find; knock
and it will be opened to you. For everyone who asks receives;
the one who seeks finds; and to the one who knocks, the
door will be opened.*

Matthew 7:7-8 (NIV)

DO WE PRAY TO FATHER GOD FOR THE TRAFFIC LIGHT TO
turn green, or do we pray to Him to keep the traffic light red? I suppose
it depends what you are praying for and whether He wants you to move
forward or wants you to wait.

I remember having an exceedingly difficult and frank conversation
with my support worker, that I was over £300 in debt. I was pregnant
and had a part-time job. It was mind-blowing. How do I pay all that back
when my income is lower than my debt? What do you do then? Curse
God or pray to Him? A lot of people blame God when things go wrong
in their lives. The world blames Him when things go wrong, but our God
is a loving, compassionate Father.

In my situation, when I realised I was in debt, instead of cursing
Father God I plugged into His love. I prayed and prayed and prayed. All
we can really do is pray. All we can do is learn to pray and be still in His
presence. Then we have peace whatever the circumstances, because
Father God is in control and will help us when we need it.

'Lord, please help me. I don't know what to do. I am so afraid of the
future. I don't know what to do, how to support myself. I don't know
how to look after this baby inside of me. I need to feed myself so that he
can grow. I need you, Father. *I need you, Father.* Thank you, Father, for
your grace and love in my life.'

I prayed this over and over during my walk in the rain, proud of my
growing baby bump but frightened of what the future would hold. In the
torment of my mind I heard Father God's calm voice. He told me He
would provide for my needs and I should trust him. He gently said,
'Hannah, come to me, you are weary and burdened, and I will give you
rest.'

God gave me rest. He put it on the hearts of others to pay off this debt. I experienced Father God's love on a much deeper level that day and it gave me great hope.

I don't want to live in my own strength. I want to stay constantly plugged into Father God's love and watch Him carry me through the storm and through the calm. I want people to know that He cares and will look after their needs. Father God is not judgemental. He's a compassionate Father, who longs for His children to be in a relationship with Him. He wants us to trust Him and to live with a childlike faith. He will not abandon or reject us.

Prayer Starter

Dear Father God, please help me. Show me the way forward for I do not know where to go. I trust in you, Lord. Amen.

DAY 73

So do not worry saying, 'What shall we eat? Or what shall we drink? Or what shall we wear?' Therefore, do not worry about tomorrow, for tomorrow will worry about itself. Each day has enough trouble of its own.

Matthew 6:28,34 (NIV)

WHEN I HEARD FATHER GOD'S VOICE IN THE STILLNESS OF my mind, I knew I did not need to worry because He was looking after my needs. He would provide for me when the timing was right. God did provide for me that day when I could not pay off my debt. Various people during that six-month period in the shelter provided for me when I could not. Father extends grace to us who pray to Him and who seek His presence. The Holy Spirit goes to people and nudges them about certain people. God our Father provides for us all the time. He loves us. He wants us to be secure in His love.

If you are struggling, whether financially, emotionally or with your health, how will you react in such a situation? Do you plant your faith in humans? Or do you plant your roots firmly in God? How can He help you? Cry out to Him and He will hear your pleas and carry you through the storm. Remember, our Father God sees the bigger picture. He knows what He is doing for the glory of His kingdom.

There is a song which says, 'You never let go, you never let go of me.' And that is true; Father God never lets us go. Even if He seems to be miles away, Father is with us. In fact, we are *never* alone. We have the Father, Son and Holy Spirit with us all the time, carrying us when we cannot carry ourselves. He gives us strength when we do not have strength. Keep plugging into the source of love. Keep plugging into God, for strength, for love and for compassion. Be on the wave of love. As you love the people around you, you make a small change in the world and bring unity where there was division.

Cry out to God and He will hear your pleas. Our Father God knows our needs. May His will be done, not our will. He knows what we need, and while it might not be what we want, His perfect plan is far better. I have messed up so many times. Consequently, I want to stay plugged into

God and be in a deeper relationship with Him. I know that He will lead me forward on this journey of uncertainty and grief. Trust and obey Father God and you will bear fruit.

I want to return to my first question: do we pray for the traffic light to turn green or red? I think God has given us a brain, so that we can use it. He wants us to use it. He wouldn't want us to sit around doing nothing. Faith is about exercising our brains and acting when needed. It is about sitting still in God's presence and resting, but never retiring and never giving up.

Prayer Starter

Dear Father God, you hear my cry. Teach me to do what is right. Show me where to go. Amen.

DAY 74

But in your hearts revere Christ as Lord. Always be prepared to give an answer to everyone who asks you to give reason for the hope you have. But do this with gentleness and respect.

1 Peter 3:15 (NIV)

IF LIFE COULD BE LIKE A TREE, FIRMLY ROOTED TO ITS PLACE, with an unwavering faith, then wouldn't life be plain-sailing and easy? Or would it be boring?

My life is generally plagued by insecurities stemming from the hurt of a forgotten past. I often feel that I am a failure. I feel that I am not wanted and that I am not loved. This is one of my biggest struggles and it became even harder after my little boy died. I felt like it was my fault. I had to learn to forgive myself. I have to remember who I am in Christ. My identity is in Christ and not in material things or in other people.

Ultimately, life is what we make of it. It is a choice we have. I know I don't want to be trapped on the treadmill of endless questions. I want to be free of them; I want to surrender them so that I can move on with my life. I had to release those questions and let them go so that they would not consume me and make me a bitter person.

Do we decide to let fear hold us down, or do we live by faith? I choose the latter. I will not let fear conquer me. If I live by fear, I will go through the following emotions: depression, isolation, self-pity, bitterness, self-hatred, and many other negative feelings. If I live by faith, I know that there is hope and that I can climb any mountain that seems insurmountable.

We have a choice to make when we face those emotions. Do we ignore our insecurities and let them fester? Or will we battle our insecurities with our shield of faith? Let's put on our garment of praise and worship God. Worship, reading God's word and prayer – those are our weapons that we can use to win the war on insecurities ravaging our souls.

It is well with your soul. *It is well with your soul.* Hallelujah!

Prayer Starter

Thank you, Father, for your love towards me. Father, thank you for the people you put on our paths that help us to refocus our eyes on you. Thank you for carrying me through the storms and through the calm. Thank you for guiding me. Father, I pray that you will help me to overcome my insecurities and that I may feel secure in the knowledge of your love. Amen. Hallelujah!

DAY 75

*Hope deferred makes the heart sick, but a longing fulfilled is
a tree of life.*

Proverbs 13:12 (NIV)

IT IS SO EASY TO FEEL DISAPPOINTED BY CIRCUMSTANCES OR by being let down by people. Disappointment is, in a way, caused by setting yourself up for failure. Better not to have expectations because when your expectations don't meet what you are expecting it leads to disappointment...

Life can take us on random adventures. You plan something for months, only to become disappointed by the outcome. 'I guess it wasn't meant to be.' In the end, God knows what is best for us. Sometimes, in the most unexpected moments, you hear Father God's voice and then you have to take courage and follow what you believe He is telling you.

I am a broken woman, suffering a host of different emotions whichever way I turn or go. My somewhat fragile mind struggles against the forces that bombard my soul – and yet somewhere deep within me I have God my Father's peace. His love and compassion are in me. God is my refuge, my shelter in times of trouble. When everything around me is falling apart, I place my trust in Him. My identity is in Christ, not in the circumstances around me or in other people. God is in control of my life, and whatever happens, He knows what is best for me. God's good and perfect plan prevails.

The enemy likes to feed us lies, telling us that God does not know what is best for us. The enemy does not like us to have peace, and destroys relationships. The enemy tells us that we have failed somehow. But the reality is, we have not failed. We have to learn to live by God's grace and to lean on Him for everything. We have to learn to plug into His source of strength. When we don't plug into that source, then we are fighting a losing battle. Is your identity in other people or in the image of Jesus? Where do your disappointments stem from?

Prayer Starter

Dear Father, please help me to let go of my expectations, my disappointments. Help me to trust you, Father, and help me to see clearly even when the paths are not straight. I will trust you. I will seek your presence. Amen.

DAY 76

*We can rejoice, too, when we run into problems and trials,
for we know that they help us develop endurance. And
endurance develops strength of character, and character
strengthens our confident hope of salvation. And this hope
will not lead to disappointment. For we know how dearly
God loves us, because He has given us the Holy Spirit to fill
our hearts with His love.*

Romans 5:3-5 (NIV)

HOW CAN YOU OVERCOME DISAPPOINTMENT? WHAT IF YOU don't overcome it? In that case, you become hostage to grief for the rest of your life. It is better to give your disappointment to God, than to internalise it. When you bury something alive, it will come to haunt you years later and erupt like a volcano. Let go of your disappointment. Trust God to help you to overcome it. Speak to Him about your disappointment but don't internalise it, because it will party in your soul like an unwelcome guest.

God promises us that those who seek Him will lack no good thing. Seek His presence. Pray to Him. Worship Him. Read scripture to pray and break free from disappointment. Allow Father God's love to seep through you.

By keeping our eyes on God, we can overcome disappointment. By believing that He knows what is best for us, we can overcome disappointment.

Forgive those who have disappointed you. Forgive yourself if you have disappointed yourself. This will enable you to be free. Give it to God; he can handle your disappointment. If you don't give it up, it can become a habit, which turns it into a besetting sin, which can lead you to be easily discouraged. You end up in a negative cycle of self-pity and don't know how to get away from it.

You could write your disappointments down on a piece of paper and then tear them up. It is an exercise of realising the pain of disappointment that consumes you, and enables you to be free. You are deliberately giving your heart more room for Father God's love with this action. In turn you can extend this love to the various relationships in your life.

Prayer Starter

Dear Father, please help me to overcome my disappointment. Help me to release it so that I can be free. Amen.

DAY 77

The Lord is close to the broken-hearted; he rescues those
whose spirits are crushed.

Psalm 34:18 (NIV)

WITHOUT BROKENESS HOW CAN WE EXPEREINCE THE SAL-vation of God? How can we demonstrate the compassion, love and healing power from God our Father? When we feel broken, we become more dependent on Him. We seek His presence because this is ultimately where we feel securely safe from prying eyes. Being broken is not something we should be ashamed of, but something that we should embrace. At the core of our brokenness we meet God, and He knits us back whole into the person He intended us to be.

If I am feeling broken, crushed in spirit, or just generally in the pit of despair, I do not want to spend time with people. I cannot cope with their superficial concern. I need substance. I need to spend time in the presence of Father God to feel whole. I need to spend time in His presence to feel the peace that I cannot find anywhere but at His table. I long for that secret place where He can just fill me with His love and show His genuine concern for me. When I am there, I don't have to be ashamed because God shows me His mercy, compassion, love, grace and so much more. If I am broken, I want to experience peace, so the sanctuary is the right place to be. It's a safe place, where I can unveil myself at the foot of the Cross, and I don't have to pretend that I am strong all the time.

...the peace of God which passes all understanding and will
guard your hearts and minds in Christ Jesus.

Philippians 4:7

Peace comes from spending time with Father God. Surrendering your shame and your brokenness at the Cross and letting Him take over, brings peace. It is about letting Him show you the way forward. In your weakness, His strength will make you strong.

God uses our brokenness. He can turn our brokenness into something beautiful for the glory of His kingdom. Simply put, your most effective ministry will come out of your deepest hurts surrendered to Him.

Prayer Starter

Dear Father God, help me to overcome my brokenness. Turn it into something beautiful. Use me as your vessel for the glory of your kingdom. Amen.

DAY 78

...and to know this love that surpasses knowledge – that you
may be filled to the measure of all the fullness of God.

Ephesians 3:19 (NIV)

REJECTION IS A SPIRITUAL BONDAGE. IT IS WHERE WE FEEL
unloved, unworthy and abandoned. Rejection has a lot of things to
answer for. It destroys our self-esteem. It destroys who we are, by making
us feel insecure to the point that we cannot cope with what life has
thrown at us. It attacks the purpose that God has set out for us. The
feeling of rejection can destroy relationships, snow us under and silence
the desires and longings that God has put in our hearts. It whispers
poisonous, insidious lies of the enemy, and it can destroy us if we do not
face it in a healthy manner.

When my son Sebastian died back in 2014, I felt like God my Father
was rejecting me. I felt as if He was punishing me, as if He thought I
would be a terrible mother. I felt punished and deeply wounded that my
son had been taken away.

Rejection brings out a lot of other negative emotions within us. For
example, we feel unworthy, abandoned, rejected, like a failure – there are
a whole host of issues. Rejection becomes a bondage. We become chained
if we don't realise or understand what scripture truly tells us. God teaches
us about love, and that He loves us conditionally. If we cannot
understand this fundamental piece of information in the Bible, then we
are set up for a life of bondage to rejection. We become slaves to it.
Fortunately, there are ways to overcome it, ways to conquer this negative
spirit and to be fully free from it.

It is amazing how many people suffer from rejection. If you want to
be all that God wants you to be, then overcoming this is vital. Replace
the lies from the enemy with truths from the Bible.

Father God looks into our hearts and wants to love us. But if there is
no room in our hearts for His love to infect us then how can we be free?
We need to learn to let go of all those negative emotions and we need to
stop believing the lies of the enemy. Plug into the source of love: God our
Father. Learn to accept that you are loved. Learn to resist the urge to ask,

'*Why* does He love me?' Accept. Accept. Accept. Pure love is infectious. Once you have experienced it, you will want more of it, because it brings a deeper peace inside of you.

Prayer Starter

Dear Father God, you made a way through the sea for your people. You opened the waters and dried out the ground, so that they could escape the enemy of rejection that was pursuing them. Do the same for me, I pray. Amen.

DAY 79

*Keep your lives free from the love of money and be content
with what you have, because God has said, 'Never, will I
leave you; never will I forsake you.'*

Hebrews 13:5 (NIV)

HOW CAN WE OVERCOME THE SPIRIT OF REJECTION?
Defeating rejection is all about identity and what you base your identity
on. For example, if you base your identity on what your parents think of
you, you are setting yourself up for rejection. You feel it the moment they
show a sign of disapproval towards you, whether it is because of the life
choices you make or something as simple as making a small mistake. This
is why it is so important to remember that we should not base our identity
on what people think of us, or even what we think of ourselves, but on
what Father God thinks of us. He says that He will never leave us and
that He will never reject us. This is the truth and it speaks volumes. This
is our hope.

The devil wants us to believe that God will reject us, and lies that He
will abandon us. Nowhere in the Bible does it say that God will reject us.
When we learn to replace the negative emotional wounds from a broken
past with positive truths from the Bible, we become bulletproof to
rejection. We can learn to become immune to the wounds of rejection if
we do not base our identity on what other people think of us.

Simply get your identity from the word of God, *not* from other
people. If reading the word of God isn't enough for you to overcome the
spirit of rejection, I would recommend that you seek help from a godly
Christian counsellor who can help you discover the roots of your
rejection. Perhaps go to a homecoming week and learn all about Father
God's love for you.[15] Once you have a counsellor, find a sanctuary where

---

[15] See *The Homecoming: Finding Your Place in Father's Heart*. The revelation
of the homecoming is about finding our place in Father's heart, finding our
home and security in His love. It's about living and experiencing Father's
love on a daily basis. More information is available at:
http://www.fathershouseeurope.com/homecoming-retreats

you can nail all your struggles to the Cross and experience renewal and wholeness at a whole new level. It is not a quick-fix solution, but it is a process, and it is hugely beneficial. You will feel free once you consciously make a choice to 'let go and let God'. He can help you to face the issues of rejection when you are open to receiving His help.

Prayer Starter

Dear Father, please help me to overcome the spirit of rejection. Help me to plug into your love. Help me to unclutter my heart, so that there is room for more of your love and less of all the negative baggage. Amen.

Cry Baby, Cry

Cry, baby, cry out the pain.
Tear the pain away from
Your heart.
Tear the scars away with your
Past.
Away they fly into nothingness.
Go to dreamland and
Sink into warm cushions of love.
Dream on – safety is on her way.
Weep heaps of water
As the past slips away with the stream.
Cry, baby,
Cry, baby,
Cry.

DAY 80

*And the God of all grace, who called you to his eternal glory
in Christ, after you have suffered a little while, he will
himself restore you and make you strong, firm and steadfast.*

1 Peter 5:10 (NIV)

SOMETIMES YOU HAVE TO BE LIKE A CHAMELEON AND adapt to the new situation as quickly as a chameleon can change to a different colour. Only it isn't as simple as it seems. It is hard. It requires us to have a certain sense of acceptance of the new situation and it can take a while to adapt. With a lot of reassurance, encouragement and support the adaptation process can be quicker and more pleasant.

I struggle with sudden change, especially since Sebastian died. When something suddenly changes, I get taken back to when my world was falling apart. I get taken back to that room where they told me my son had passed on, and the room was spinning completely out of control. I find that when there is a sudden change, my body reacts negatively, although that reaction can be hard to put into words. It is probably my body's way of protecting myself from further hurt, from further disappointment. It is my body's way of trying to protect myself from what it perceives as a threat.

How do you cope with sudden change? Do you cope with it OK? Or do you shy away from it? Do you feel trapped, or as though you are losing control of the situation? Have peace, for God is in control and you can overcome the insurmountable mountain by and through His strength.

Prayer Starter

Dear Father, please help me to be at peace today as I learn to adapt to my new situation. Father, help me, please, to cling onto the Cross. Help me to be the person you created me to be. Lead me beside still waters. Thank you for giving me peace. Thank you, Lord, for being in control. Thank you for loving me. Thank you for the situation you give us where we can seek to trust you again, and again, and again. Thank you, Father. Amen. Hallelujah!

DAY 81

*May the Lord Jesus Christ himself and God our Father, who
loved us and by his grace gave us eternal encouragement and
good hope encourage your hearts and strengthen you in
every good deed and word.*

2 Thessalonians 2:16-17 (NIV)

'DISCOURAGEMENT' IS DEFINED AS A LOSS OF CONFIDENCE
or enthusiasm. We are all prone to discouragement at some stage in our
lives. However, some of us are more prone to it than others. I often feel
discouraged when things don't go according to my plan. But ultimately,
it is God's plan that is best for us. It is His plan that will prevail. God
does not like us to feel discouraged. If it becomes a habit, it will become
hard to break free from.

What causes discouragement?

- *Fatigue.* When you are emotionally and physically exhausted you
  will be more prone to discouragement, as your defences are
  weaker, and you are at your most vulnerable.
- *Frustration.* When unfinished tasks pile up, it is natural to feel
  overwhelmed. Sometimes day-to-day life gets in the way of
  completing tasks. Then frustration can easily sneak in. This makes
  you more vulnerable to discouragement, which infects us like the
  plague.
- *Failure.* When you plan something and the plan disintegrates, you
  react negatively. You let self-pity hog you. You feel like a failure
  which lets discouragement creep in stealthily – between the cracks
  of your façade of confidence.
- *Fear.* Fear is everywhere. It is behind a lot of discouragement. We
  are afraid of criticism, and when we get criticism, we feel
  discouraged because we don't know how to react to it positively.

Is there a cure for discouragement? I encourage you, whenever you
feel discouraged, to seek God's presence and pray to Him. Surrender your
struggles to the Cross, so that you can be free. Learn to speak positive
affirmations over yourself according to scripture. Don't let the devil make

you become hostage to discouragement. Be free. Choose to let go of the negativity around you. Choose to let Father God's love be the essence of who you are, and not all that negativity around you. Choose to have a relaxed attitude when things don't go according to plan. Learn to praise God in the storm as well as through the calm. He is there, carrying you. You can be free when you learn to be content in all circumstances. Hallelujah!

Prayer Starter

Dear Father, please help me to overcome discouragement. I need your help to let go of everything that is tearing me apart. Amen.

DAY 82

You are my fortress in times of trouble.

Psalm 59:16 (NIV)

SHORTCUTS SEEM WELCOMING BUT CAN BE DEADLY. THERE was a time when I was trapped in the rising floodwaters of grief and I just wanted it all to end. A shortcut seemed like a welcome escape. I just wanted to be in a different time, in a different space. I wanted the end result.

I did not want to go through the process or on the journey to healing. I wanted a quick fix. I wanted to take a shortcut because if I did, the grief would curl around my body and take hold of me and I'd be stuck inside its tightly clenched fist. I would be begging, 'My God, my God, please do not forsake me.' If I didn't grieve it would become all-consuming. Tiresome. Wearisome. Painful, to say the least.

I learnt with time that grief has to be lived out, not to be avoided. I learnt that you alone can walk through your pain, with the Father, Son and the Holy Spirit holding you when you can't walk further. If you don't walk through grief, in pain, it will come back to haunt you many years later. My worst nightmare is being trapped in grief, being held hostage to it.

Though grief has sat with me since the death of my boy, it does not control my life. It does not need to control your life either. Grief has taught me much. But it no longer overwhelms me as it did in the beginning because I learnt to surrender this to God. I learnt to let Him love me and comfort me when no-one else could. I learnt to let Him carry my grief.

I have hope now. I can see light. My hope is in Him. God is my stronghold. He is my rock and my refuge. In Him I seek my shelter. In Him I find my dwelling place.

If you know someone who is going through spiritual battles, the greatest gift you can give them is your love, your time, your attention, your concern, your safe touch. That is my challenge. I want to reach out to others and help them face the uncertainties of the unknown murky waters of flooding grief. Just knowing that someone is there by your side, encouraging you from the cheering line, can help you come to a place of acceptance and peace much more quickly. God has blessed me. Though I have lost my child, I am blessed, because through this tragedy I have learnt one fundamental lesson: *God is grace.* God is love. God loves me. God accepts me with all my faults. I am His and He dwells in me.

Prayer Starter

Dear Father God, please do not allow me to take a shortcut on this journey of grief. Help me to take the journey before me and teach me not to be afraid. Amen.

DAY 83

A relaxed attitude lengthens the life.

Proverbs 14:30 (NIV)

ALL MY LIFE I'VE HAD SO MUCH ANGST INSIDE OF ME. I OFTEN feel that peace is an elusive commodity. It comes and goes like a butterfly passing by. When I am filled with angst, I struggle to talk to God my Father; I don't know where to begin. Yet he knows my every thought; He has X-ray vision. God knows my every fear, He knows every detail about me, and that is a comforting thought. So, even when I don't talk to God out loud, I am sure that He can hear me and my silent anger and see my heart of stone.

My fear of abandonment and rejection is very real. It is a spiritual stronghold in my life that I am trying to overcome. It stems from my childhood when my parents divorced. Divorce is never healthy for children. It brings up a whole host of issues and often scars you. But you can heal from it. Subsequently, I struggle with a multitude of emotions from a lifetime of hurt. I no longer want to live like this. I want to be plugged into the constant stream of Father God's love and radiate His love to everyone I speak to. When I am plugged into Father God's love, I am free, I am at peace, I feel complete.

I realise now more and more that I need to anchor my hope in God and that I need to be fully dependent on Him. He knows my future. He knows your future. God is in control of it, not us. So, if we are trying to be in control of our future, it will just lead to a mess. Allow God to be in control, allow Him to take the lead. Learn to trust Him blindly. All of us are broken. We need to fix our hope and trust in God, not in worldly goods. This is my daily prayer.

When I feel that my emotions will erupt like a volcano, I bring my struggles to the Cross, to Father God. I read through encouraging scriptures that I have written down in my little book so that peace can seep into my heart of stone. I am learning to live by faith. I am learning to relax. I am learning to take risks. I am learning to be loved even though it scares me because I do not want to get hurt again.

Risks are worth it. Fear is not. Do not let yourself live in fear, because it robs you of your joy and peace and the promises of Father's kingdom. Live by faith. Trust God. Believe that He will meet your needs. Stay plugged into His constant stream of love. Stay on the wave of love. Learn to accept yourself. Let go and let God.

Prayer Starter

Dear Father God, help me to accept myself. Teach me to live by faith and not by sight. Help me to let go and let you in. Amen.

DAY 84

For God so loved the world that He gave his only son to die,
so that we may have eternal life.

John 3:16 (NIV)

HAVE YOU LOST SOMETHING DEAR TO YOU? HAVE YOU LOST
children but do not talk about it? Do you find that you are lost in a world
that doesn't seem to make sense at all? Do you question what your
purpose in life is; what is the meaning of life; what is the point in living
when there is so much pain in the world, so much sadness? Do you
wonder where God is in all of this? I have questioned God countless times
about my purpose: what is my purpose, what does God want me to do
with my life?

Recently I read that grieving parents do not get over it and they don't
move on. I disagree with that statement. Grieving parents *can* get over it
and *can* move on if they allow God to heal them. They can bring their
feelings to the foot of the Cross and ask God to bind up their wounds.

The same goes for any issue that you have in life. You *can* heal from
it. You *can* let it go; you don't need to hold it. It does not need to define
who you are. It can shape you as the person you are, but it does not need
to consume you. Let God heal you.

Why do people want to be stuck in a state of overwhelming sadness
for the rest of their lives? I am not trying to judge anyone. I am trying to
encourage you. Both God and your lost loved one want you to move
forward. Yes, it hurts, when you have lost someone or something you
deeply love. Yes, it hurts, not having the thing that you have lost. But
don't let that stop you from living your life to the fullest. Don't let your
sadness and grief overwhelm you to the point where you are merely
existing, not living.

Jesus came to take away our pain and grief so that we can live. He
took away our suffering so that we can live again. Yet, it is a conscious
choice that *you* have to make. Do you want to be stuck in grief or do you
want to be free? Most of the time tragedy occurs for no reason and you
have to accept it, even if that feels like an impossible feat. Jesus will help

you. Father God will help you. He will love you all the time through the storm and through the calm. Give Him your struggles.

Prayer Starter

Dear Father, I want to let go of my sadness and trust that you can heal me. Help me to be free; heal me from the pain of my past. Amen.

DAY 85

But if we hope for what we do not yet have, we wait for it patiently.

Romans 8:25 (NIV)

HAVE YOU EVER EXPERIENCED *DÉJÀ VU* MOMENTS BETWEEN your reality and your dreams – a familiar gap between your dreams you are working towards and your present reality, which you have been in before? Then comes a sudden painful realisation – the nagging gap you are experiencing now is one you don't want to be in again…

Sometimes you just want to press the fast-forward button, like you can when watching movies. Wouldn't it be a great invention to be able to press the fast-forward button to get to the place you want to be in – the moment where your dreams and the reality you are in merge together and become what you want it to be?

The problem with this, if we fast-forward, is that we will be skipping vital life lessons that God wants to teach us. There is no fast-forwarding ticket to where we want to be, no fast-forward button to get you off the grief train. You must simply wait patiently. You should work towards your goal patiently and if you really want it to happen, then make it happen. Seek God's word, pray to Him. Include Him in your plans – don't exclude Him.

Sometimes Father God has a different plan for us. Does it mean that sometimes you have to let go of a certain dream so that another dream may take its place? If it is God's plan, then yes.

We dream to give ourselves hope. Being hopeless means living in darkness. Having hope means living in light. To have hope means that the Holy Spirit has planted a seed, a desire inside of you, that one day may grow to become a flourishing true story. But for that to happen you need to ask if you have the courage to pursue your dreams. Do you have the courage to follow God's perfect and pleasing plan? Do you trust Him to work everything out for your future? After all, it is God who is in control. When He is in charge of your life, all is well, and nothing is impossible because God has got your back.

Prayer Starter

Dear Father, please help me to have the patience to wait and the courage to move forward and to take risks. Help me to have the courage to follow your perfect and pleasing plan for my life.

DAY 86

*For it is by grace you have been saved, through faith – and
this is not from yourselves, it is the gift of God – not by
works, so that no one can boast. ... He came and preached
peace to you who were far away and peace to those who
were near. For through him we both have access to the
Father by one Spirit.*

Ephesians 2:8-9,17-18 (NIV)

HOW DO WE WORSHIP GOD IN THE STORM? HOW DO WE
praise our Holy Father when we are faced with severe opposition? Do
you want to praise God? Or do you just want to lie about feeling sorry
for yourself?

I often wake up grumbling and feeling sorry for myself. I am
wallowing in self-pity and self-obsessed. I worry about my appearance
and about what others might think of me. I experience very low self-
esteem, and self-loathing for the bad choices I have made in my life. I
continue to be self-conscious. Is this a way to live life? Is it good to
grumble and to argue with yourself and to hate yourself? Why not learn
to accept who you are in the image of Christ?

Jesus taught us:

*Love the Lord your God with all your heart and with all
your soul and with all your mind and with all your strength.
... Love your neighbour as yourself.*

Mark 12:30-31

Is it not important what God thinks of me, rather than what the world
thinks of me? I am not of this world, but of Father God's kingdom.
Kingdom living according to His will means we must delve deeper into
scripture, sit in His presence and actively seek to hear His word, His voice
inside us.

It is a constant battle between the flesh and the spirit. But let God's
spirit prevail and help your spirit win. Don't succumb to your flesh. Let
the Holy Spirit enable you and guide you to make the decisions in your
life. Allow yourself to feel God's presence. Allow yourself to be loved. Sit

still with Him. Be still, instead of rushing around. Take your time; look outside at the beauty of the world, at our Father God's creation. Don't be frightened to sit in His presence. He is a compassionate God and loves to spend time with you.

Prayer Starter

Dear Father, please help me to love myself. Help me to love you with all my heart and all my soul. Help me to be content in all circumstances whatever may pass. Amen.

DAY 87

*Do everything without grumbling, so that you may become
blameless and pure, 'children of God without fault in a
warped and crooked generation.' Then you will shine among
them like stars in the sky.*

Philippians 2:14-15 (NIV)

AFTER SEBASTIAN DIED, I MADE A CONSCIOUS DECISION TO wear the garment of praise and to worship my Father God instead of falling into the devil's snare. My saviour is the only one who has the key to my soul and can heal the deepest wounds in my heart. Although a few people have helped to stop the bleeding, it is ultimately God who can restore us to our whole wellbeing. Realising this, I made a conscious effort to talk to my Father God and to Jesus my saviour. He is the only one who knows every thought that goes through my head. It is scary that He knows everything. and yet it is oddly comforting. I am not alone during the fierce battles of my mind. In fact, I am never alone. My God is always with me. Believe that our three-in-one God is also with you.

I have been saved by the grace of God countless times. I know I don't deserve it, but God does not see us as sinners. He sees us as little lost children who need him. Father God saved me and took me home so many times. I was rescued. My emergency call was answered and help arrived at my doorstep. He carefully carved a hole in my heart, so that He could infect me with his contagious love. He heard my cry in the darkness of the night, heard my deep heartache and comforted me. I bring my brokenness to Him so that I can be healed in His presence.

The depth of Father God's love runs deeper than ocean trenches and the gaping chasms in our lives. It runs through our very veins. We have to accept it, keep learning to accept it, and to live by faith. This means trusting and obeying God with all our heart and with all our might.

Prayer Starter

Dear Father, please help me to accept your love and not be afraid of it. Help me to declutter the mess in my heart, so that there is more room for your love. Come, Father, into my heart, heal my brokenness. Amen.

DAY 88

*My grace is sufficient for you, for my power is made perfect
in weakness. Therefore, I will boast all the more gladly about
my weaknesses, so that Christ's power may rest on me. That
is why for Christ's sake, I delight in weaknesses, in insults, in
hardships, in persecutions, in difficulties. For when I am
weak, then I am strong.*

2 Corinthians 12:9-11 (NIV)

'MY GRACE IS SUFFICIENT FOR YOU!' ISN'T THAT A POWERFUL
line of scripture? It should be an encouragement to us to cling onto Father
God in our weaknesses. After all, where does our strength come from?

It is the foolish things of this world that shame the wise.[16] I learnt
over the years that too many Christians are afraid to proclaim what God
has done in their lives and not share to the world the good news of His
grace and love. I learnt that we should not be afraid to share what God's
grace has done in our lives.

There is nothing wrong with boasting about what God has done for
us, how He carried us through difficult periods. In fact, God wants us to
share this with the world, so that we can give others hope. If we do not
share what God has done during our difficult times, during our grief
journey, how will people know of His power, of His love, of His
compassion? If we deny that God gave us the strength and courage to
overcome the grief journey, then where will all those other lost souls go
to? Should we not be proud that God helps us 24/7 whatever the
circumstances?

God our Father wants us to share our stories with the world, so that
we can give hope to others.

After my little boy died, I started writing to express my grief.
Eventually, God would use my writing to help others. He wants to show
others that His grace is sufficient for me, for you, for all.

It is quite simply really – all you have to do is share what God has
done and in return you will be blessed. We all have a ministry. God wants

---

[16] See 1 Corinthians 1:27

us to show people that there is hope. We demonstrate to others in our darkness that there is light for them in difficult circumstances, and that through our weaknesses God makes us strong. He is with us throughout everything because He loves us.

Prayer Starter

Dear Father God, help me to boast gladly about what you did for my life and how you met my needs. Teach me your ways to overcome difficulties. Let light in. Amen.

Day 89

Nevertheless, I will bring health and healing to it; I will heal my people and will let them enjoy abundant peace and security.

Jeremiah 33:16 (NIV)

FATHER DOES NOT WANT HIS PEOPLE TO SUFFER. HE WANTS us to rest in his presence and feel the transforming power of peace that he so generously wants to give to all the nations on earth.

But healing doesn't usually occur overnight. It is a process. You need to be willing to step into the centre of the storm, so that you can experience God's grace and love abundantly. Then you can witness His healing power. It is about surrendering your struggles to the Cross, so that you can be free. It is about allowing all the negative emotions inside you to be released and replacing them with the word of God. God's promises and truths from the Bible bring affirmation.

After Sebastian died, I would have to regularly unburden myself at the foot of the Cross. I needed to feel Father God's healing power on my very broken soul. It was a question of endurance and patience: do I want to go into the centre of the storm, or will I run away from it and not face it?

Part of accepting my son's death was learning to forgive myself. For a long time, I blamed myself for his death. I felt that it was my fault, that I should have done more to save him. But the endless treadmill of 'What if I had done this?' or 'What if...?' does us no good. It just digs us into a deeper hole of despair, depression, anger, frustration and unforgiveness which can create a root of bitterness inside of us.

If we want to be free, we need to be willing to accept the reality that we are still alive. We can choose to surrender our issues at the foot of the Cross rather than creating a one-year, two-year, ten-year, even forty-year deep pit of despair. What will you do? Surrender your struggles at the foot of the Cross? Or bury them deep within you till they fester into an angry ball that can ignite at a moment's notice?

Prayer Starter

Dear Father, thank you for your love. Thank you for the comfort you provide me when I have nowhere to turn. Thank you for your healing, and for lifting me up when I can't move forward. Help me, Lord, to endure this grief and not bury it. Amen.

Perseverance

When all the world is looming dark
And things are clouded darkly,
I lean onto Father for
Understanding and direction in my life.
When I feel like I am falling,
Falling, you whisper a gentle
Message of hope and encouragement
In my ear, Father, because
You love me even though I do not
Deserve it.
When I feel like there is no other way
And feel the darkness curl around me,
You remind me to keep going,
To keep putting my full trust in you.
When I want to slam the door,
You keep opening it gently
And I trod this path even if I
Feel the pain echoing in my heart.
You whisper that I am not alone
And that you take the pain from
My shoulders.
I learn to talk to you again, O Father,
Without a doubt or fear that
Surrounds my aching soul
Somehow, I feel that things will be OK
And so I keep persevering in
The safety of Father's love,
My dwelling place.

DAY 90

*And the God of all grace, who called you to his eternal glory
in Christ, and after you have suffered a little while, will
himself restore you and make you strong, firm and steadfast.*

1 Peter 5:10 (NIV)

GOD USES THE WILDERNESS PERIOD TO STRIP US OF ALL THE
superficial layers. He reveals to us what is really in our hearts. Will we
curse Him in our time of troubles? Or will we praise him even when we
are facing death, like the psalmist David did? What do you do when you
are going through a difficult time? Do you run hundreds of miles away
from God? Or do you praise Him and allow Him to heal your broken
wounds and make you whole?

Before my son died, I would run a hundred miles away from God. I
did not think that He could help me solve my problems. I did not think
God would want to hear from me, because I always came to Him when
things were tough. But over time, I learnt that our Father wants us to rely
on Him all the time; He is there for us regardless, through thick and thin.
God wants to be with us. He wants us to have a relationship with Him.
Our Father God hates seeing His children suffer.

When Sebastian died, I remember deliberately thanking God for the
circumstances I was in and praising his name. This was tough. But I was
showing God that He was my number One in life, and that He was far
greater than any problem or tragedy in my life. By doing this, I was
enabling myself to go on a healthy grief journey, rather than becoming
trapped in it. I was allowing Father God to heal me, comfort me, at what
would have been the hardest time of my life. I was opening the door for
Him to enter and heal what was broken.

During this time, I learnt to read the Bible daily, to study scripture,
to write down encouraging scriptures, and just to talk to God each day.
I surrendered my struggles to the Cross, as they were too heavy for me to
carry alone. As I did, Father God helped me to heal. He showed me that
there was hope when I thought there was none.

Prayer Starter

Dear Father, thank you for your love, thank you for giving me the experiences I needed to make me the person I am now. Help me to heal; help me to focus on you and not on myself. Amen.

DAY 91

I am with you always, to the end of age.

Matthew 28:20 (NIV)

GOD SAYS, 'I WILL BE WITH YOU.' WHATEVER CIRCUMSTANCE we find ourself in, whether it is in the middle of a storm or in the most peaceful, joyful time of our life, God is with us. God is everywhere. He never leaves us, nor does He forsake us.

When Sebastian died, I remember feeling like I was alone in the world. When my mum left the hospital room, the sense of isolation overwhelmed me. My mum had gone, my dear Sebby had gone. I felt so deeply wounded.

But when I think back to that time, I realise that I was not alone. I see Father God's hand in it. He was in the room with me when the doctor told me Sebby had died. He was with me when I lay there by myself, in silence, staring at the machine that was measuring my contractions and my son's non-existent heartbeat. God was with me through it all. I was so deeply hurt; I felt rejected, frightened, unsure of what the future held for me. I wept bitter tears of regret – tears of deep pain and grief – for all that was to be but was no longer.

Father God was in that very hospital room with me, meeting my needs and comforting me, even if I did not know. I look back and wonder how else could I have managed to get through those days if it was not for Father God's comfort, love and the people He so strategically placed around me. If God was not there in those early days after my Sebastian died, I would have surely perished and turned my back on Him, because I just couldn't cope with it. Father God knew. In fact, He carried me through those early days, cradled like a baby in His arms, as I did not have the energy to crawl. I didn't have the energy to do anything.

I was afraid to be stuck in grief, so I spent a lot of time in solitude singing praises to God, thanking Him for the circumstances I was in, and not letting my son's death be futile. I refused to let the devil win. God gave me the courage to face the wilderness, so that I could come out of it and speak of His great love for us. I can now share with the world the assurance that God never leaves us. We simply have to let Him into our lives and not be afraid. We just need to learn to pray and spend more time with Him.

Prayer Starter

Dear Father God, thank you for not forsaking me. Thank you for always being there. Amen.

DAY 92

My God is my rock, in whom I take refuge,
my shield, and the horn of my salvation.
He is my stronghold, my refuge, and my saviour –
from violent people you save me.

2 Samuel 22:3 (NIV)

GOD OUR FATHER SAYS, 'I WILL PROTECT YOU.' WE ARE SAFE, not because of the absence of danger, but because we are in the presence of God our Father. He delights in His children who cling to Him, who search for Him and make Him a refuge. He grieves for those who are lost and longs for them to come near to Him. Father God wants us to go to Him so that we can experience peace in times of trouble. If we call out to the Lord, He will meet our needs and save us from danger. He protects us in whatever circumstances we find ourselves. But we have to understand that going through trials is part of living in a fallen world.

When my son died, Father God protected my faith, by showing me His love for me, by comforting me. Sometimes we go through trials in life so that we can draw closer to God. The trials of life can purify us and draw us closer to Him.

Sometimes being protected from the trials of life is not in our best interest. This is because it is through such trials that we can grow in our Christian walk, become more spiritually mature and learn to have perseverance, whatever the trial is before us.

How do we receive Father God's protection? It is only through developing a personal relationship with Him that we will experience His protection. That means praying. Yes – praying, praying, praying; studying scripture, worshipping the Lord and being in fellowship with others, so that we can experience His protective arms around us.

Remember, Father God does not want us to suffer. He wants us to grow in faith, and sometimes we need to go through fire to learn more about Him. In that way God is preserving and protecting us from further damage. Trust Him and He will set all things right before us.

Starter Prayer

Dear Father, please do not forsake me as I go through the trials of life. Help me to face my fears, and help me to feel safe in the comfort of your arms. Amen.

DAY 93

The Lord is my strength, and my defence; he has become my salvation.

Psalm 118:14 (NIV)

'I WILL BE YOUR STRENGTH,' SAYS GOD. ISN'T THAT A GREAT promise from our Father – a fantastic gift? I often ask myself this question: 'Where does my strength come from? How have I overcome this insurmountable mountain?'

Some people may think that we have to put back together the broken puzzle pieces of our lives by ourselves. But when you look at the bygone time, and how far you have come, you begin to realise that God's hand was in it. You know God was your strength in your weakest moment and carried you through.

When times are tough, whom do we rely on? Do we rely on God? Or do we rely on our own strength? Our built-in instinct tells us to become more dependent on God. He uses suffering to bring us close to Him. He says, 'Run to me, and my grace will carry you home.' His love is sufficient for us. In our weakness He makes us strong and gives us courage to overcome the trials we face.

In Him, I will find my rest. But in finding my rest I should humble myself before Him. I should learn to surrender my struggles to the Cross so that I can be free. By doing that, I also have to acknowledge that I am not living on my own strength, but by the Holy Spirit who lives in me. He gives me the strength to keep persevering, even when I want to give up. God's Holy Spirit gives us the courage to face adversity in our lives and gives us the strength to overcome it.

Often, we do not want to acknowledge that the strength we receive is from our Father God. Once we learn to acknowledge that He gives us the strength to overcome our difficulties, then we can begin to testify to others about His goodness towards us for the glory of His kingdom.

Prayer Starter

Dear Father God, help me to proclaim the good news even in times of trouble, for my faith is in you. Amen.

DAY 94

*He will call on me, and I will answer Him, I will be with him
in trouble, and I will deliver him and honour him.*

Psalm 91:15 (NIV)

GOD SAYS, 'I WILL ANSWER YOU.' THIS IS WITHOUT A DOUBT true. God answers us even when we are not always aware that He is answering us or His answer might not be what we want. For example, I remember praying to God for the *perfect father* for my son. I was hoping I would get married and then in turn my son would have a father who would be good to him. Of course, when Sebastian died, I was grief-stricken. I blamed myself for a long time for my son's death, for praying that wrong prayer. I thought because I prayed that prayer, God didn't think I was a good enough mother. But the truth is, God answers us even when we don't realise that He has. It is not always how we want it to be answered. But I know now that God is in control.

When I was in the pit of despair, I called out to Father God and He heard me; He pulled me out of the pit and He bound up my open wounds. He met me in that dark place and held me, guided me to the high rock where I could find my rest. God met me and comforted me when no-one else would, when I was at my lowest low. He would speak to me through my writing, through music and through my art.

You need to believe that God can answer you. He provides for all of us. He answers us when we seek His face. We do not have to be afraid to seek His face, even when we are angry at our situation. Sometimes when we are angry with Him, God just pours out His love to us. He does not condemn us for being angry. His answer is love. His love is sufficient for us to get through the difficult time, and that is an answer – even when we want something else, something more. God says, 'Ask and it will be given to you.' God answers us in the most unimaginable ways possible. We just have to believe and have faith and be open to hearing from Him. Just look at the miracles all around you.

Prayer Starter

Dear Father, help me to hear your voice, even when you seem so far away. Help me to be open to what you have to say. Amen.

DAY 95

I have received full payment and have more than enough. I am amply supplied, now that I have received from Epaphroditus the gifts you sent. They are a fragrant offering, an acceptable sacrifice, pleasing to God. And my God will meet all your needs according to the riches of his glory in Christ Jesus.

Philippians 4:18-19 (NIV)

GOD SAYS, 'I WILL PROVIDE FOR YOU.' I HAVE WITNESSED God's provision for me countless times in the past, and right now. It goes without saying, if we are doing His will, God will care for our needs and provide for us so that we are able to fulfil our purposes for the glory of His kingdom.

When I was thinking of publishing my first book, *Sebby – Son of Hope,* I had no financial means, and lacked faith that the book could become a credible story. But I knew that it was in God's will for the book to be published. I prayed that He would provide financially for me to do this. Sure enough, He provided the resources for the book's publication.

This was astounding for me. I had thought, 'Can God really provide for the likes of me?' The answer was yes!

God provides for His children, whatever our needs. We can pray and He will provide for us so that we can accomplish His will for the glory of His kingdom. Remember, though, that God won't provide what we requested if He believes that it is not good for us. He will not provide anything that might harm us.

We often take things for granted. This is especially true when God provides for us such things such as food or a roof over our heads. This seems a very simple thing, but in fact this is a daily miracle. God wants to provide for His children, but He also wants us to seek His presence. He desires we ask of Him, commune with Him and surrender our struggles to Him. Father God wants us to be free. He wants us to trust Him in all things. It is often hard to believe that God will carry us through the storm and provide for our needs, but He will.

Prayer Starter

Dear Father, help me to trust you as you provide for me during my time of grief, and always. I will trust you and seek you. Amen.

DAY 96

Now may the Lord of peace himself give you peace at all times and in every way. The Lord be with you all.

2 Thessalonians 3:16 (NIV)

FATHER GOD WILL GIVE US PEACE. WHEN THE HOLY SPIRIT dwells within you, you will receive the peace of God that surpasses all understanding.

When Sebastian died, I remember very clearly that I had the peace of God within me. I don't know where it came from, but I was at peace despite the overwhelming tragedy that was staring me in my face and the long grief journey that lay ahead of me. *Father God was with me.* I could feel His presence very clearly. He helped me to go through those first few dark days after I was told my son was longer to be.

God gives His people peace if we learn to lean into Him for protection and comfort. He wants us to surrender our struggles so that we do not have to carry them on our shoulders or be burdened by them. He wants us to be free and to experience His transforming peace.

To experience peace, we must let go of our struggles and our grief. Then we can let His peace, love, compassion, grace and mercy wash over us till we experience healing inside.

This is not always easy, as we need to be dedicated to spending time with God until He comes and presents us with peace. He gives us peace and joy to deal with affliction. He gives us patience to deal with affliction and to not fear the unknown. But it requires discipline and trusting Him for guidance.

Here is a simple tip: learn to surrender your struggles at the foot of the Cross, and Father God will give you His everlasting peace whatever the circumstances. In the good and in the bad, His peace reigns. Hallelujah!

Prayer Starter

Dear Father God, help me to surrender. Thank you for your peace. You are faithful, and I trust in you and I love you, Lord. Amen.

DAY 97

And now these three remain: faith, hope, and love. But the
greatest of these is love.

1 Corinthians 13:13 (NIV)

GOD WILL ALWAYS LOVE US. HE DOES NOT VIEW US AS sinners; this is our perception of ourselves. He sees us as lost children. Although we view ourselves as sinners, we are saved by His grace. He engulfs us with His love.

God loved us so much that He let His only Son die for us so that we may have eternal life. How amazing is that!

Life is challenging but with God's help we will pull through the tough moments. He does not like to see us suffer. However, He can use our situations of suffering to draw us close to Him so that we can experience His unconditional love.

God does not ask us to be perfect. If His love were conditional, we would be constantly seeking His approval. We would be looking at what we need to do to earn it. But because it is unconditional, we do not have to be perfect. We simply have to accept God's love and to trust Him that He knows what is best for us. Even if we think that the situation we are in is awful, we still trust our loving Lord is with us in it and through it.

God did not banish us to the wilderness. He simply uses the wilderness time as a place to draw us near to Him. He strips the superficial from us to reveal what is truly in our hearts. Are we going to praise the Lord even when times are tough? Or are we going to turn away from Him and curse Him because He is putting us through a difficult time?

My biggest comfort after Sebastian died was this simple fact: Jesus died so that we may have eternal life. How much more painful must it have been for our Father God to lose His only Child so that we may have eternal life? In that way I realised my suffering is minuscule compared with Father God's suffering when his Son died so that I could have eternal life. Even though I am a sinner, for Father God I am just a lost little girl who is saved by His grace.

How did our Father God overcome the loss of His Son?

Prayer Starter

Dear Father God, thank you that I can come to you for comfort. Thank you for taking away my pain. Thank you for your love. Amen.

DAY 98

Return to your stronghold, O prisoners of hope, today I
declare that I will restore to you double.

Zechariah 9:12 (ESV)

WAIT ON THE LORD, BE OF GOOD COURAGE AND HE SHALL strengthen your heart. The grief journey can be a long one, but if we put our focus on God then ultimately, we can hold onto hope. We become bound to hope.

We live in a time of turmoil, affliction, spiritual warfare and much more, but we don't have to lose hope, because we know that God will see us through the difficult moments in life. He will guide us to a platform of safety. That is our hope yesterday, today, tomorrow and forevermore.

When we suffer, what matters is how we react to the situation. Do we react to it with a godly attitude or do we react in an ungodly way? Do we condemn God for putting us in that situation?

It is hard to praise the Lord in tumultuous times, but God is far greater than our problems. Our God is a magnificent God, who can help us to overcome anything that we face. He can transform us. But we need to place our trust in Him. We need to believe and trust in Him that He will pull us through a time in which we have become hostage to mediocre problems in our day-to-day life.

Yes, grief can keep us captive, sometimes for more than forty years, sometimes only a few years. But what is the correct response in the face of a trial? Do we lash out at God and question why He inflicted punishment on us? A trial can feel like punishment. But is it punishment? Or do we choose to trust our Father God?

Where does your hope lie? Does it lie with other people? Or does your hope come from God?

Prayer Starter

Dear Father, please let me become bound to hope, and not a prisoner of grief. Amen.

DAY 99

There are different kinds of gifts, but the same Spirit
distributes them. There are different kinds of service, but the
same Lord. There are different kinds of working, but in all of
them and in everyone it is the same God at work.

1 Corinthians 12:4-6 (NIV)

HAVE YOU EVER QUESTIONED GOD ABOUT THE PURPOSE OF your very existence? Or have you asked Him why you have gone through, so much trial and tribulation? Have you ever said things like this to yourself: 'Can God use my suffering for the glory of His kingdom, I wonder? Does God give me gifts and talents so that I can help others after I have gone through trials and tribulations?'

I've always felt that I was inept and not worthy of receiving gifts from the Holy Spirit. I also believed that I wasn't a good Christian. I saw myself as one of those Christians who made mistake after mistake after mistake, while the other good Christians around me never made any blunders. Or so it seemed!

Maybe I saw that they never made blunders because they always wore a mask of 'perfection' and a mask of 'I am a good Christian and I do not make mistakes'. They also wore an 'always happy' mask, thinking that because they were Christians, they couldn't display their weakness and vulnerability in trouble, tribulation or trials.

This may be the reason why I believed mask-wearing people were quick to judge me. I was quick to criticise myself and to judge myself, which made it difficult for people to like me because they were afraid of my vulnerability. I didn't make it easy for them to come near me. Maybe it was simply because I had built a *huge* wall around my heart so that people could not come near me because I was afraid of getting hurt.

I needed to learn to 'let go and let God'. God revealed Himself to me, and said, 'Hannah, this is not the way forward. Be yourself, let go of your struggles and use your writing to reach people.'

I want to be Father's little girl. I have no desire to do everything in my own strength anymore, because I know that my way does not work. I know that my plans do not work. It is God's plans that work and are best for me, so I surrender my struggles to Him. I disarm myself and I de-clutter everything so that I can live a simple life. I don't want my life to be complicated. God is simple. Why? Simply, because God is love. God is love, God is mercy, God is compassion, God is grace, God is forgiveness, God is a giver. God wants us all to have gifts and talents that we can use so that we can glorify His kingdom and bring non-believers to Him. He wants us to serve Him.

As for me and my household, we will serve the Lord.

Joshua 24:15

Jesus needs more and more labourers as the harvest is ripe. Are you ready to use your gifts and talents to serve our Father?

Prayer Starter

Dear Father God, help me to let go of my struggles. Help me to help others. Help me to sing of your goodness all my days. Amen.

Teasing Grief

Waves in and out crashing against the hardened shell
Of a woman lost in a world between cheer and grief,
Toying with her emotions like the wind plays with her hair,
The glimmer of tears hammering briefly behind her eyes
As if ready to let the gushing waterfall of deep woe flow out
Into the endless rivers filled with droplets
Of a forgotten past.

O, my child, where has time gone to?
Teasing grief always sitting stifling a giggle
Behind its hand, ready to lure me into
The dark pond of grief, where familiar shapes
Fill my mind, reminders are strewn across
Haplessly as I cling onto a twig
Only for it to be nearly ready to collapse under pressure
Of the forceful river that carries
My every emotion into the rolling
Carpets of a time gone by.

O, my child; o, my child
Thousands upon thousands of tears were shed
For you, still thousands upon thousands of tears
Await to spill. Forgive me, Lord,
For my weakness, my fragile state of mind.
How I wish upon a star, and wish I could
Have held you...
Except you are safe now,
Safe in the arms of Jesus
While teasing grief sits on my shoulder
Toying with my fragile emotions.
Should I weep? Should I not weep?

DAY 100

*'Love the Lord your God with all your heart, and with all
your soul and with all your mind and with all your strength.'
… 'Love your neighbour as yourself.'*

Mark 12:30-31 (NIV)

TODAY I'M MEDITATING ON HOW ABBA FATHER DESIRES US
to be in relationship with Him, and it inspires me. Just learning about
Abba's love makes me realise how infectious and contagious His love is
for us.

I want more of Abba's love in my life. I want to be plugged into His
love. I never want to be unplugged from it. I desire to delve deeper and
deeper into His love. I want to be my Father God's daughter. I want to
be His little girl, and I want this constant stream of love. His love is
amazing – absolutely amazing – and such a huge blessing to my life. It
brings great peace to my heart, and reassurance that it is well with my
soul. It is a wonderful feeling knowing how loved I am, how much my
Father God loves me, how many of my Christian brothers and sisters love
me. I am experiencing how my spiritual family loves me. I am in awe at
what an amazing Father in heaven we have. I now know we are not
sinners in Father God's sight but His little children.

All my life I have believed that I was a sinner, that I am not worthy
of love. But the revelation of Father God's love has opened my eyes and
given my spirit hope. I believe there is hope in the world and that love
can win. I now understand that God's love can open the eyes of so many
people and give people so much peace – if we are genuinely open and
ready to receive it.

We as Christians should spread this love to the nations and show
them what a wonderful Father we have in heaven. There should be no
division between us. We need to start loving each other, and we need to
stop believing the lies of the enemy. We need to start believing our self-
worth in God the Father.

I want to be a living example of the love that God has for me. I want
it to radiate from me to the world. I want to spread this love to the world,

and I want to bring hope to so many people and show them the light where they only see darkness.

I used to be afraid of love, but I think I would rather take the risk of being loved than miss out on the most basic human need: LOVE. I will take this risk. Hallelujah! May you be blessed as you navigate your life's journey with God by your side.

Prayer Starter

Dear Father God, thank you for your goodness. Thank you for leading me on this dark journey. Thank you for not forsaking me. Thank you that I can trust in you. Thank you for healing me. Amen.

The Memory of Trees

I don't want to walk through the puddles of life.
Hopscotching between the edges of sharp rocks,
Kissing the green trees, holding hands,
Trust and faith go hand in hand;
Water rushing, flowing in and out of the folds
Of rocky green mountains,
Trees, the guiding lamp of hope and strength.
Sitting beneath the bending branches
On a tree stump of serene rest,
My heart flutters at the sweet
Melody of birds, at the memory of trees;
Splintered hope of minty moss,
Slanted trees lying on a hot bed of dark green.
It's the beginning of beauty beyond the eye,
Life a miraculous bloom of colour,
Sprouting life and song.
Standing on the edge of morning misty dew,
My heart sings of hope and peace.
I am whole; at last I am whole.

Final Thoughts

WHEN I STARTED WRITING THIS BOOK IN EARLY 2017, I WAS still in the midst of grief. However, healing took place slowly but surely with godly counsellors, and friendships formed. Early on in my grief journey I thought I would never smile again, let alone laugh. Now I seem to laugh all the time and can hear the echo of it bouncing off the walls. Live and learn. Life is too short for us to stay in a continuous cycle of grief. While I learned a lot from grief, I also am learning to live again, to laugh again, and for me this means to be free in Christ. It means freedom in Christ.

God is good. He never left my side, and I believe that as you continue on this journey of grief to Hope Restored, God will journey alongside you. He will take some steps for you while He holds you in His arms. But this one thing I know without a doubt: He will never forsake or abandon you. He will always be near.

I've also learned since that mourning is a process and that through the mourning process you gain wisdom on the way so that you can help others on the same journey. As the bible says:

It is better to go to a house of mourning than to go to a
house of feasting, for death is the destiny of everyone; the
living should take this to heart.
Ecclesiastes 7:2

If I hadn't lost my son or gone through the various challenges that were presented to me, I would never have gained the wisdom that God desired me to have. Embrace grief, allow it to take you on a journey of self-reflection, revelation and much more. Allow yourself to experience God's love on a whole new level. Don't be afraid of it. God will guide you with His light on the path that He has chosen for you.

I look back over the years and I know one thing for sure is this: I don't regret everything that I have experienced. I am glad that God chose me to experience those things, because in a way it has made me stronger and given me strength of character. Don't allow yourself to be deterred from how difficult the journey will be because ultimately from out of the ashes comes joy.

Be encouraged. May the Lord bless you on your journey.